THE SILENCE OF GOD

THE SILENCE OF GOD

by
Sir Robert Anderson

KREGEL PUBLICATIONS
Grand Rapids, Michigan 49501

THE SILENCE OF GOD, Copyright © 1978 by Kregel
Publications, a division of Kregel, Inc. All rights reserved.

Library of Congress Cataloging in Publication Data

Anderson, Robert, Sir, 1841-1918.
  The Silence of God.

  (Sir Robert Anderson library)
  Reprint of the 8th ed. published in 1907 by
Hodder and Stoughton, London.
  1. Christianity—19th century. I. Title
II. Series: Anderson, Robert, Sir, 1841-1918.
Sir Robert Anderson Library.
BR121.A57   1978   231   78-9528
ISBN 0-8254-2128-4

Printed in the United States of America

First Kregel Publications edition 1978
Reprinted 1981

CONTENTS

vi / Contents

PUBLISHER'S PREFACE

God has remained silent now for almost two thousand years. No new prophets have arisen and the voice of God has not orally spoken since He spoke to His Beloved Son. Why?

Sir Robert Anderson approaches this problem with his usual methodical and complete investigation and findings. God is not revealing any new truths, because the Scriptures are already complete; and God has said all He intends to say to this present generation. God has closed His revelation to man in the Bible in spite of the claims of those who would have us believe otherwise.

"There is no new thing under the sun," cried Solomon in Ecclesiastes. Yet, our generation cries out that there is new "revelation" from God and that the authority of our Bible needs to be supplemented with the teachings of these new "prophets of God." The last hundred years have produced several different "prophets" that have introduced supposedly new revelations from the Heavenly Father. Strangely, however, each of the new prophets has introduced revelation that differs from that which the Bible states God has already revealed.

Though written many years ago, the arguments and facts revealed here are still timely and much needed. As long as the Lord Jesus delays His return, there will continue to be the rise of false prophets, and there will be the continued need of this book: that we may KNOW that God has already spoken, and that revelation is complete.

The Publishers

PREFACE TO SEVENTH EDITION

IN again reissuing *The Silence of God* I wish to make a few points clearer for the benefit of those who skim a book instead of reading it.

I do not deny the occurrence of miracles during the present dispensation. On the contrary I believe there is adequate proof that miracles occur in the present day. And while I would guard against assuming that a miracle gives proof of *Divine* action, I do not doubt that there are in fact Divine miracles. Nor in saying this am I referring to spiritual miracles such as every true Christian has experienced.

But I maintain that what may be called *evidential* miracles have no place in this " Christian dispensation." Any one who thinks out even the simple problem of prayer must understand how and why the people of God, in the days before Christ came, craved such proofs of His presence and power. But in the ministry and death and resurrection of the Lord Jesus Christ God has openly manifested, not only His power, but His goodness and love-toward-man; and to demand an evidential miracle, now, is to reopen questions which have been for ever settled.

No one may limit what God will do in response to faith. But we may dogmatically assert that, in view of the revelation He has given of Himself in Christ, He will yield nothing to the petulant demands of unbelief. And that revelation supplies the key to the double mystery of the silence of Heaven and the life of faith on earth. R. A.

PREFACE TO SECOND EDITION

IN his introduction to *The Scarlet Letter*, Nathaniel Hawthorne descants feelingly upon his incapacity for literary effort during the years in which he held an appointment in the Custom House. But there are spheres of work in the Public Service compared with which the Custom House might seem almost a sanctuary! And having regard to the circumstances in which the present volume was written, the demand for a new edition within a few weeks of its first appearance gives striking proof of deep and widespread interest in the subject of which it treats.

Conflicting criticisms have been passed upon the structure of the book. In the opinion of some the middle chapters embarrass the argument, and ought to be omitted or curtailed. Others, again, have strongly urged that these very chapters should be amplified, and definite additions made to them. These seemingly contradictory suggestions are both alike legitimate. To a very limited class such incidental dissertations seem unnecessary, and the mere critic turns from them with impatience; but in the estimation of the great majority of readers they are of exceptional interest. The ninth and eleventh chapters, for example, which might perhaps have been excluded, seem to have attracted special notice.

It must not be forgotten, moreover, that, unlike those doctrines which belong to the Christian dispensation in common with that which preceded it, the great characteristic truth of Christianity is ignored by the religion of Christendom, and receives but scant attention even in our best religious literature. It is of vital moment, therefore, to unfold here its character and scope, and to emphasise its transcendent importance. Indeed it will probably be found that the reader's appreciation of the argument will be precisely in proportion to his apprehension of this truth.

One of the leading daily papers, for instance, informs its readers that the author "finds the sufficient cause of the silence in the doctrine of the Atonement." And another journal—a Review of the highest class [1]—indicates as the "main contention" of the book, "that the Christian facts supply an adequate explanation of the 'Silence of God.'" It might *a priori* seem impossible that any one could so misread these pages ; but the preceding paragraph may perhaps account for the phenomenon. "The Atonement" is not a specially *Christian* doctrine at all : it holds as prominent a place in Judaism as in Christianity. And the author's "contention," most plainly expressed, is that "the Christian facts," so far from explaining the silence of Heaven, seem only to render it still more inexplicable.

In the judgment of this last-cited critic the intensely Protestant and Christian position maintained throughout this volume is nothing more than a "peculiar view of Scripture as a supreme

[1] "Literature."

guide in matters of faith and speculation." And writing from the standpoint this indicates, his strictures are, of course, unsympathetic and severe. Nor can the author complain of this ; for one who deals hard blows should expect hard blows in return. But there should be no "hitting below the belt." The impartial reader can decide whether these pages afford even a colourable pretext for the charge of "occasional departures from reverence." And no less unwarrantable is the allegation that Mr. Balfour is here referred to in "a patronising tone." Considerable freedom, indeed, is used in criticising the arguments of a still more distinguished man. But the author's misgivings upon that score have been relieved by receiving a letter from Mr. Gladstone himself. "I am very glad," he writes, "that those arguments should be thoroughly canvassed by persons so well disposed and competent as yourself."

39, LINDEN GARDENS, W.

1

THE SILENT HEAVEN

A SILENT Heaven is the greatest mystery of our existence. Some there are, indeed, for whom the problem has no perplexities. In a philosophy of silly optimism, or a life of selfish isolation, they have "attained *Nirvana*." For such the sad and hideous realities of life around us have no existence. Upon their path these cast no shadow. The serene atmosphere of their fools' paradise is undisturbed by the cry of the suffering and the oppressed. But earnest and thoughtful men face these realities, and have ears to hear that cry ; and their indignant wonder finds utterance at times in some such words as those of the old Hebrew prophet and bard, "Doth God know? And is there knowledge in the Most High?"

Society, even in the great centres of our modern civilisation, is all too like a slave-ship, where, with the sounds of music and laughter and revelry on the upper deck, there mingle the groans of untold misery battened down below. Who can estimate the sorrow and suffering and wrong endured during a single round of the clock even in the favoured metropolis of highly favoured England? And if it be thus in the green tree, what shall be said of the dry! What mind is competent to grasp the sum of all this great world's misery, heaped up day after day, year after year, century after century? Human hearts may plan, and human hands achieve, some little to alleviate it, and the strong and ready arm of human law may accomplish much in the protection of the weak and the punishment of the wicked. But as for God—the light of moon and stars is not more cold and pitiless than *He* appears to be!

Every new chapter in the story of Turkish misrule raises a fresh storm of indignation throughout Europe. The conscience of Christendom is outraged by tales of oppression and cruelty and wrong inflicted on the Christian subjects of the Porte.

Here is a testimony to the Armenian massacres of 1895 :

" Over 60,000 Armenians have been butchered. In Trebizond, Erzeroum, Erzinghian, Hassankaleh, and numberless other places the Christians were crushed like grapes during the vintage. The frantic mob, seething and surging in the streets of the cities, swept down upon the defenceless Armenians, plundered their shops, gutted their houses, then joked and jested with the terrified victims, as cats play with mice. The rivulets were choked up with corpses ; the streams ran red with human blood ; the forest glades and rocky caves were peopled with the dead and dying ; among the black ruins of once prosperous villages lay roasted infants by their mangled mothers' corpses ; pits were dug at night by the wretches destined to fill them, many of whom, flung in when but lightly wounded, awoke underneath a mountain of clammy corpses, and vainly wrestled with death and with the dead, who shut them out from light and life for ever.

" A man in Erzeroum, hearing a tumult, and fearing for his children, who were playing in the street, went out to seek and save them. He was borne down upon by the mob. He pleaded for his life, protesting that he had always lived in peace with his Moslem neighbours, and sincerely loved them. The statement may have represented a fact, or it may have been but a plea for pity. The ringleader, however, told him that that was the proper spirit, and would be condignly rewarded. The man was then stripped, and a chunk of his flesh cut out of his body, and jestingly offered for sale : ' Good fresh meat, and dirt cheap,' exclaimed some of the crowd. ' Who'll buy fine dog's meat ? ' echoed the amused bystanders. The writhing wretch uttered piercing screams as some of the mob, who had just come from rifling the shops, opened a bottle and poured vinegar or some acid into the gaping wound. He called on God and man to end his agonies. But they had only begun. Soon afterwards two little boys came up, the elder crying, ' *Hairik, Hairik* (Father, father), save me ! See what they've done to me ! ' and pointed to his head, from which the blood was streaming over his handsome face, and down his neck. The younger brother—a child of about three—was playing with a wooden toy. The agonising man was silent for a second and then, glancing at these his children, made a frantic but vain effort to snatch a dagger from a Turk by his side. This was the signal for the renewal of his torments. The bleeding boy was finally dashed with violence against the dying father, who began to lose strength and conscious-ness, and the two were then pounded to death where they lay. The younger child sat near, dabbling his wooden toy in the blood of his father and brother, and looking up, now through smiles at the prettily dressed Kurds and now through tears at the dust-begrimed thing that had lately been his father. A slash of a sabre wound up his short experience of God's world, and the crowd turned its attention to others.

"These are but isolated scenes revealed for a brief second by the light, as it were, of a momentary lightning-flash. The worst cannot be described."—*Contemporary Review*, January, 1896.

The following refers to still more recent horrors :

"In no place in this region has the attack upon the Christians been more savage than in Egin. Every male above twelve years of age who could be found was slain. Only one Armenian was found who had been seen and spared. Many children and boys were laid on their backs and their necks cut like sheep. The women and children were gathered together in the yard of the Government building and in various places throughout the town. Turks, Kurds, and soldiers went among these women, selected the fairest, and led them aside to outrage them. In the village of Pinguan fifteen women threw themselves into the river to escape dishonour."—*The Times*, December 10, 1896.

And what is the element in all this which most

exasperates the public sentiment? It is that the Sultan has the power to prevent all this, but will not. That, while possessing ample means to restrain and punish, he remains unmoved, and in the safe seclusion of his palace gives himself up to a life of luxury and ease. But has Almighty God no power to check such crimes? Even Abdul Hamid has been shamed into laying aside the dignity of kingship, and making heard his personal voice in Europe to repel the charge his seeming inaction has raised to his discredit.[1] But in vain do we strain our ears to hear some voice from the throne of the Divine Majesty. The far-off heaven where, in perfect peace and unutterable glory, God dwells and reigns, is SILENT !

"So I returned, and considered all the oppressions that are done under the sun; and behold, the tears of such as were oppressed, and they had no comforter ; and on the side of their oppressors there was power ; but *they* had no comforter." And this in a world ruled and governed by a God who is Almighty !

[1] The Marquis of Salisbury's speech at the Pavilion, Brighton, on the 19th of November, 1895.

And when we withdraw our thoughts from the great world around us, and fix them upon the narrow circle of His faithful people, the facts are no less stern, and the mystery grows more inscrutable. Devoted men leave our shores, forsaking the security, the comforts, the charms, the countless benefits of life in the midst of our Christian civilisation, to carry the knowledge of the true God to heathen lands. But by and by we hear of their massacre by the hands of those whom thus they sought to elevate and bless. And where is "the true God" they served? The little band of Christian men who were in a special sense His accredited ambassadors, noble women too, who shared in their exile and their labours, and little children whose tender helplessness might excite the pity of a very devil, in their terror and agony cried to Heaven for the succour which never came. The God they trusted might surely have turned the hearts, or restrained the hands, of their brutal murderers. Is it possible to imagine circumstances that would more fitly claim the help of Him whom they worshipped as all-powerful both in heaven and on earth? But the earth has drunk in their blood, and a silent Heaven has seemed to mock their cry!

And these horrors are but mere ripples on the surface of the deep, wide sea of the Church's sufferings throughout the ages of her history. From the old days of Pagan Rome right down through the centuries of so-called "Christian" persecutions, the untold millions of the martyrs, the best and purest and noblest of our race, have been given up to violence and outrage and death in hideous forms. The heart grows sick at the appalling story, and we turn away with a dull but baseless hope that it may be in part at least untrue. But the facts are too terrible to make exaggeration in the record of them possible. Torn by wild beasts in the arena, torn by men as merciless as wild beasts, and, far more hateful, in the torture chambers of the Inquisition, His people have died, with faces turned to heaven, and hearts upraised in prayer to God; but the heaven has seemed as hard as brass, and the God of their prayers as powerless as themselves or as callous as their persecutors!

But most men are selfish in their sympathies.

Some private grief at times looms greater than all the sum of the world's miseries and the Church's sufferings. If ever there was a saint on earth, it is the mother to whose deathbed sons and daughters have been summoned from various pursuits of business or of pleasure. In all their wanderings that mother's piety and faith have been a guiding and restraining influence. And now, thus gathered once more in the old home, they are keen to watch how, in the solemn crisis of her last days on earth, God will deal with one of the loveliest and truest of His children. And what do they behold ? The poor body racked with pain that never ceases till all capacity for suffering is quenched by the hand of Death ! If human skill could give relief the attending physician would be dismissed as heartless or incompetent. Is *God*, then, incompetent or heartless ? To Him they look to relieve the death agonies of the dying saint, but they look to Him in vain !

Or it may be some grief more selfish still. The crash of some great sorrow that turns a bright home into a waste, and leaves the heart so benumbed and hard that even the so-called " consolations of religion " appear but hollow platitudes. Why should God be so cruel? Why is Heaven so terribly silent?

The most prolific fancy, the most facile pen, would fail to picture or portray, in their endless variety, the experiences which have thus stamped out the last embers of faith in many a crushed and desolated heart. " There are times," as a Christian writer [1] puts it, " when the heaven that is over our heads seems to be brass, and the earth that is under us to be iron, and we feel our hearts sink within us under the calm pressure of un-yielding and unsympathising law." How true the statement, but how inadequate! If it were merely on behalf of this or that individual that God failed to interfere, or on one occasion or another, belief in His infinite wisdom and goodness ought to check our murmurs and soothe our fears. And, further, if, as in the days of the patriarchs, even a whole generation passed away without His once declaring Himself, faith might glance back, and hope look forward, amidst heart searchings for the cause of His silence. But what confronts us is

[1] Dean Mansel.

the fact, explain it as we may, that for eighteen centuries the world has never witnessed a public manifestation of His presence or His power.

"Doth God know?" At first the thought comes up as an impatient yet not irreverent appeal. But presently the words are formed upon the lip to imply a challenge and suggest a doubt ; and at last they are boldly uttered as the avowal of a settled unbelief. And then the sacred records which awed and charmed the mind in childhood, telling of "mighty acts" of Divine intervention "in the old time," begin to lose their vividness and force, till at last they sink to the level of Hebrew legends and old-world myths. In presence of the stern and dismal facts of life, the faith of earlier days gives way, for surely a God who is entirely passive and always *unavailable* is for all practical purposes non-existent.

2

THE MYSTERY REMAINS

WHEN we turn to Holy Writ this mystery of a silent Heaven, which is driving so many to infidelity, if not to atheism, seems to become more utterly insoluble. The life and teaching of the great Prophet of Nazareth have claimed the admiration of multitudes, even of those who have denied to Him the deeper homage of their faith. All generous minds acclaim Him as the noblest figure that has ever passed across the stage of human life. But Christianity claims for Him infinitely more than this. The great and unknown God had dwelt in impenetrable darkness and unapproachable light — seeming contradictories which harmonise in fact in a perfect representation of His attitude toward men. But now He at last declared Himself. The Nazarene was not merely the pattern man of all the ages, He was Himself Divine, "God manifest in the flesh." The inspired prophets had foreshadowed this : *now* it was accomplished. The dream of heathen mythology was realised in the great foundation fact of Christianity—God assumed the form of a man and dwelt as a man among men, speaking words such as mere man never spoke, and scattering on every hand the proofs of His Divine character and mission.

But the sphere of the display was confined to the narrowest limits—the towns and villages of a district scarcely larger than an English county. If this was to be the end of it, a theory so sublime must be exploded by its inherent incredibility. But throughout His ministry He spoke of a mysterious death He had to suffer, and of His rising from the dead and returning to the heaven from which He had come down, and of triumphs of His power to follow upon that ascension—triumphs such as they to whom He spoke were then incapable of understanding. And, in keeping with the hopes He thus inspired, among His latest utterances, spoken after His resurrection and in view of His ascension, we find these sublime and pregnant words—" All power is given unto Me in heaven and on earth." The position of avowed unbelief here is perfectly intelligible ; but what can be said for the covert scepticism of modern Christianity which explains this to mean nothing more than the assertion of a mystical authority to send out preachers of the gospel !

Accept the scheme of revelation as to man's apostasy and fall, and his consequent alienation from God, and the history of the world down to the time of Christ can be explained. But type and promise and prophecy testified with united voice that the advent of Messiah should be the dawn of a brighter day, when " the heavens should rule," when all wrong should be redressed, and sorrow and discord should give place to gladness and peace. The angelic host who heralded His birth confirmed the testimony, and seemed to point to its near fulfilment. And these words of Christ Himself ring out like a proclamation that earth's great jubilee at last was come. Nor did the events of the early days which followed belie the hope.

If because of a great public miracle wrought by them in His name the apostles were threatened with penalties, they appealed from men to God, and then and there God gave public proof that He heard their prayer, for "the place was shaken where they were assembled." [1] Sudden judgment fell upon Ananias and Sapphira when they sinned, and as a consequence "great fear came upon all." [2] "By the hands of the apostles were many signs and wonders wrought among the people." [3] From the surrounding villages "the multitude"—that is the inhabitants *en masse*—gathered to Jerusalem carrying their sick, "and they were healed *every one*." [4] And when their exasperated enemies seized the apostles and thrust them into the common prison, "the angel of the Lord by night opened the prison doors and brought them forth." [5]

At this very period it was, no doubt, that the martyr Stephen fell. Yes, but ere he sank beneath the blows showered upon him by his fierce murderers, the heavens were opened, and revealed to him a vision of his Lord in glory. If martyr-

---

[1] Acts iv. 31.   [2] Ibid. v. 1–11.   [3] Ibid. v. 12.
[4] Ibid. v. 16.   [5] Ibid. v. 19.

dom brought such visions now, who would shrink from being a martyr! By a like vision the most prominent witness to his death became changed into an apostle of the faith he had resisted and blasphemed. And when he in his turn found himself in the grasp of cruel enemies at Philippi, his midnight prayer was answered by an earthquake which shook the foundations of his prison. Unseen hands struck off the chains which bound him, freed his feet from the stocks in which they had been made fast, and threw the gaol doors open.

The Apostle Peter, too, had experienced a like deliverance when held a prisoner by Herod at Jerusalem, and this on the very eve of the day appointed for his death. The record is definite and thrilling. "Peter was sleeping between two soldiers, bound with two chains; and the keepers before the door kept the prison, and behold the angel of the Lord came upon him, and a light shined in the prison; and he smote Peter on the side and raised him up, saying, Arise up quickly. And his chains fell off from his hands." "The iron gate" of the prison "opened to them of its own accord," and together they passed into the street.

These are but gleanings from the narrative of the opening chapters of the Acts of the Apostles. Divine intervention was no mystic theory with these men. "All power in heaven and on earth" was no mere shibboleth. The story of the infant Church, like the early history of the Hebrew nation, was an unbroken record of miracles. But there the parallel ends. Under the old economy the cessation of Divine intervention in human affairs was regarded as abnormal, and the fact was explained by national apostasy and sin. And the times of national apostasy were precisely the period of the prophetic dispensation. Then it was that the Divine voice was heard with increasing clearness. But in contrast with this, Heaven has now been dumb for eighteen long centuries. This fact, moreover, might seem less strange if prophecy had ceased with Malachi, and miracles had not been renewed in Messianic times. But though miraculous powers and prophetic gifts abounded in the Pentecostal Church, yet when the testimony passed out from the narrow sphere of Judaism, and was confronted by the philosophy and civilisation of the heathen world—at the very time in fact when, according to accepted theories, their voice was specially required—that voice died away for ever.

Is there nothing here to excite our wonder? Some of course will dispose of the matter by rejecting every record of miracles, whether in Old Testament times or New, as mere legend or fable. Others again will protest that miracles are actually wrought to-day at certain favoured shrines. But here in Britain, at least, most men are neither superstitious nor infidel. They believe the Biblical record of miracles in the past, and they assent to the fact that ever since the days of the apostles the silence of Heaven has been unbroken. Yet when challenged to account for this, they are either wholly dumb or else they offer explanations which are utterly inadequate, if not absolutely untrue.

To plead that the idea of Divine intervention in human affairs is unreasonable or absurd is only to afford a proof how easily the mind becomes enslaved by the ordinary facts of experience.

The believer recognises that such intervention was common in ancient times, and the unbeliever most fairly argues that if there really existed a God, all-good and almighty, such intervention would be common at *all* times. The taunt would be easily met if the Christian could make answer that this world is a scene of probation where God in His infinite wisdom has thought fit to leave men absolutely to themselves. But in presence of an open Bible such an answer is impossible. The mystery remains that "God, who at sundry times and in divers manners spake in time past unto the fathers," never speaks to His people now! The Divine history of the favoured race for thousands of years teems with miracles by which God gave proof of His power with men, and yet we are confronted by the astounding fact that from the days of the apostles to the present hour the history of Christendom will be searched in vain for the record of a single public event to compel belief that there is a God at all ! [1]

[1] See Appendix, Note I.

3

HAVE MIRACLES CEASED?

IN the old time men worshipped false gods, as they do still in heathendom to-day. Atheism is the recoil from Christianity rejected. But the unbelief of earnest men who are willing to believe, but cannot, is not to be confounded with the blind and bitter atheism of apostates.

Nor will it avail to plead that the miracles by which Christianity was accredited at first still live as evidence of its truth. That will not satisfy the question here at issue, which is not the truth of Christianity but the fact of a silent Heaven. That in presence of the measureless ocean of human suffering in the great world around us, and in spite of the articulate cry so constantly wrung from the hearts of His faithful people, God should preserve a silence which is absolute and crushing—this is a mystery which Christianity seems only to render more inscrutable.

Here, however, we are assuming that miracles are possible, and thus we shall incur the contempt of all persons of superior enlightenment. But we can brook their sneers. Nor will they betray us into the folly of turning aside to enter upon the great miracle controversy, save in so far as the subject in hand requires it. Open infidelity has made no advance upon the arguments of Hume. Indeed the phenomenal triumphs of modern science have only served to weaken the infidel's position, for they have discredited the theory that new discoveries in nature might yet account for the miracles of Scripture. The only thing distinctive about the infidelity of our own times is that it has assumed the dress and language of religion. Among its teachers are " Doctors of Divinity" and Professors in Christian universities and colleges. And as the disciples and admirers of these men claim for them superior intelligence and special vigour of mental perception, an examination of these pretensions may not be inopportune. But vivisection is to be deprecated, and mere abstract statements carry little weight. How, then, are we to proceed? An Oxford Professor of the past generation will do as the *corpus vile* for the inquiry. Let us turn to the treatise upon "The Evidences of Christianity" in the notorious "Essays and Reviews." Its thesis may be stated in a single sentence—That the reign of law is absolute and universal. From this it follows of course (1) that a miracle is an impossibility, and (2) that Holy Scripture is altogether unreliable. Inspiration, therefore, is out of the question, save as all goodness and genius are inspired.

It may seem feeble to turn back now to the "Essays and Reviews," but the last forty years have made no change in the German Rationalism which that epoch-making book first brought to the notice of the average Englishman. These views are being taught to-day in many of our schools of theology. The future occupants of so-called Christian pulpits are being taught that the miraculous in Scripture must be rejected, and that the Bible must be read like any other book.

Now what concerns us here is not whether this

teaching is true : let us assume its truth. Nor yet whether the teachers be honest : we assume their integrity. But what can be said for their intelligence ? Any dullard can trade upon the labours of others. The most commonplace of men can understand and adopt the tenets of the rationalists. Where mental power will declare itself is in the capacity to review preconceived ideas in the light of the new tenets. Let us apply this test to the Christian rationalists. The incarnation, the resurrection, the ascension of Christ—these are incomparably the greatest of all miracles. If we accept them the credibility of other miracles resolves itself entirely into a question of evidence. If we reject them the whole Christian system falls to pieces like a house of cards. To change the figure, when Christianity is exposed to the clear light and air of "modern thought," what seemed to be a living body crumbles into dust. Yet these men profess unfaltering faith in Christianity. But while their faith does credit to their hearts, it proves the weakness of their heads. Those who believe in the Divinity of Christ while rejecting inspiration and miracles, may pose as persons of superior enlightenment—in fact, they are credulous creatures who would believe anything. Such faith as theirs is the merest superstition. Appeal might here be made to unnumbered witnesses among the scholars and thinkers of our time, who in face of this dilemma have found themselves compelled to choose "between a deeper faith and a bolder unbelief."

If Christ was indeed Divine, no person of ordinary intelligence will question that He had power to open the eyes of the blind, the ears of the deaf, the lips of the dumb. If He had power to forgive sins, it is a small matter to believe that He had power to heal diseases. If He could give *Eternal Life* there is nothing to wonder at in the record that He could restore natural life. And if He is now upon the throne of God, and all power in heaven and earth is His, every man of common sense will brush aside all sophistries and quibbles about causation and natural laws, and will recognise that our Divine Lord could do for men to-day all He did for them in the days of His ministry on earth.

But how is it that He does not ? I know that if

in the days of His humiliation this poor crippled child had been brought into His presence He would have healed it. And I am assured that His power is greater now than when He sojourned upon earth, and that He is still as near to us as He then was. But when I bring this to a practical test, it fails. Whatever the reason, it does not *seem* true. This poor afflicted child must remain a cripple. I dare not say He *cannot* heal my child, but it is clear He *will* not. And why will He not? How is this mystery to be explained? The plain fact is that with all who believe the Bible the great difficulty respecting miracles is not their occurrence but their absence.

In his "Foundations of Belief," Mr. Balfour reproduces the suggestion that if the special circumstances in which a miracle was wrought were again to recur, the miracle would recur also. But even if the truth of this could be ascertained, it would have no bearing on the present problem. Miracles, Mr. Balfour avers, are "wonders due to the special action of Divine power." As then we have to do neither with a mere machine nor with a monster, but with a personal God who is infinite in wisdom and power and love, how is it that in a world which, *pace* the philosopher, cries aloud for that "special action," we look for it in vain?

In his "Studies Subsidiary to the Works of Bishop Butler," Mr. Gladstone speaks in the same sense, but still more definitely. In his discussion of Hume's dictum, that miracles are impossible because they imply the violation of natural laws, he says: "Now, unless we know all the laws of nature, Hume's contention is of no avail; for the alleged miracle may come under some law not yet known to us." But surely this admission is fatal. The evidential value of miracles, against which Hume is arguing, depends on the assumption that they are due, as Mr. Balfour says, to "the *special* action of Divine power," and that but for such action they would not have occurred. That is to say, it is essential that the act or event represented as miraculous should be *supernatural*. If, therefore, the "alleged" miracle can be brought within the sphere of the *natural*, it is thereby shown not be a *real* miracle. In other words, it is not a miracle at all.

If a miracle were indeed a violation of the laws

of nature, not a few of us who believe in miracles would renounce our faith. For then the word "impossible" would be transferred to the sphere in which it is rightly predicated of acts attributable to the Almighty. "It is," we declare, "impossible for God to lie": it is equally impossible for Him to violate His own laws; He "*cannot* deny Himself." But this vaunted dictum owes its seeming force solely to confounding what is *above* nature with what is *against* nature. Beyond this it is nothing but a cloak for ignorance.

Here is a stone upon the road. In obedience to unchanging law it lies there inert and tends to sink into the ground. Were it to rise from the earth and fly upward toward the sky, it would, you say, be indeed a miracle. But this you know is absolutely impossible. Impossible! A rude boy who comes along snatches it from us and flings it into the air. This mischievous urchin has thus achieved what you declared to be impossible! "But," you exclaim, "this is mere trifling, we *saw* the boy throw it up!" Is it by our senses, then, that the limits of possibility are to be fixed? This is materialism with a vengeance! Suppose the boy himself should fall over a precipice, and you grasped him and drew him up again to safety, would this be a violation of the law of gravitation ? Why, then, should it be such if his rescue were achieved by some unseen hand ? A miracle it would be, no doubt, but not " a violation of the laws of nature." As Dean Mansel expresses it, a miracle is merely "the introduction of a new agent, possessing new powers, and therefore not included under the rules generalised from a previous experience."

But some thoughtless person may still object that matter can be put in motion only by matter, and that to talk of a stone being raised by an unseen hand is therefore absurd. Indeed ! Will the objector tell us how it is he puts his own body in motion ? The power of something that is not matter over matter is one of the commonest facts of life. The Apostle Peter walked upon the sea. " Nonsense," the infidel exclaims, with a toss of his head, " that would be a violation of natural laws ! " And yet the phenomenon may have been as simple as that produced when he himself shakes his head ! It is possible, moreover, that the laws may yet be explained under which the miracles were performed.[1] Nor would they cease to be miracles if those laws were known ; for the test of a miracle is not that it should be inexplicable, but that it should be beyond human power to accomplish it. Whether or not the power in exercise be Divine is matter of evidence or inference ; but once the presence of Divine power is ascertained, a miracle, regarded as a *fact*, is accounted for.

If a surgeon restores sight to a blind man, or a physician rescues a fever patient from death, the fact excites no other emotion than our gratitude. But when we are told that such cures have been achieved by Divine power without the use of medicine or the knife, we are called upon to refuse

[1] This possibly may be what Mr. Gladstone means in the statement criticised at p. 25 *ante*. But if so, I am at a loss to understand either his language or his argument. He seems to suggest that the "alleged" miracles may yet be explained to us, just as the predicted eclipse of the moon which terrified the South Sea Islanders might afterwards have been explained to the savages. My own meaning an illustration may make plain. That fire should come down from the sky and kindle a pile of wood is a commonplace phenomenon. It might occur during any thunderstorm. But if I heap wood together upon a certain spot, and at my word lightning falls upon it and consumes it, this is a miracle ; and the element of the miraculous is in the fact that I have set in motion some power that is above nature and competent to control it.

even to examine the evidence. The plain fact is that men do not believe in " Divine power," or the "unseen hand." Disguise it as we will this is the real point of the controversy. In the case of every *human* being, " special action " is a duty if thereby he can relieve suffering or avert disaster ; but in the case of the Divine Being it is not to be expected or indeed tolerated ! It is accepted as an axiom that Almighty God must be a cipher in His own world !

The doctrinaire infidel rejects Christianity on the ground that the only evidence of its truth is the miracles by which it was accredited at the first, and that miracles are impossible—propositions, both of which are untenable. The ordinary infidel, on the other hand, bringing practical intelligence and common sense to bear upon the question, rejects Christianity because, he argues, if the Christian's God were not a myth He would not remain passive in presence of all the suffering and wrong which prevail in the world. That is to say, discarding the contention of the doctrinaire philosopher that miracles are impossible, he main-tains that if there really existed a Supreme Being of infinite goodness and power, miracles would abound. And the vast majority of infidels belong to this second category. But though the philosophers are few, and their sophistries have failed to take hold of the minds of common men, they have well-nigh monopolised the attention of Christian apologists. Common men, moreover, unlike the philosophers, are apt to be both fair and earnest, and ready to consider any reasonable explanation of their difficulties. But the answer offered them is for the most part either futile or inadequate.

Mr. Gladstone, for instance, falls back upon the plea that " if the experience of miracles were universal, they would cease to be miracles." But what possible ground is there for this? They would cease to excite wonder, no doubt; but that is no test of the miraculous. In the beginning of our Lord's ministry, and before the antipathy of the religious leaders of the Jews took shape in plots for His destruction, His miracles of healing were so numerous and so free to all, that they must have come to be regarded as matters of course. He "went about," we read, "in *all* Galilee, healing *all* manner of disease and *all* manner of sickness among the people. And the report of Him went forth into *all* Syria, and they brought unto Him ALL that were sick, holden with divers diseases and torments, possessed with devils, and epileptic, and palsied ; and He healed them." [1] In presence of such an unlimited display of miraculous power all sense of wonder must have soon died out. But yet every fresh cure was a fresh miracle, and would have been recognised as such.

And so would it be in our own day, if, for example, whenever a wicked man committed an outrage upon his neighbour, Divine power intervened to strike down the offender and protect his victim. The event would cease to excite the least surprise ; but all would none the less recognise the hand of God, and own His justice and goodness. And there would be no infidels left— except, of course, the philosophers !

The difficulty therefore remains unsolved. The true explanation of it will be considered in the sequel ; but at this stage the discussion of it is a mere digression. So far as the present argument

[1] Matt. iv. 23, 24 (R.V.).

is concerned the matter may be summed up in borrowed words: "The Scripture miracles stand on a solid basis which no *reasoning* can overthrow. Their *possibility* cannot be denied without denying the very nature of God as an all-powerful Being; their *probability* cannot be questioned without questioning His *moral* perfections; and their certainty as matters of fact can only be invalidated by destroying the very foundations of all human testimony." [1]

[1] Bishop Van Mildert's "Boyle Lectures," sermon xxi. Of the truth of these last words Hume's celebrated treatise supplies most striking proof. He takes exception to the evidence for the Christian miracles; but when he goes on to speak of certain miracles alleged to have occurred in France upon the tomb of Abbé Paris, the famous Jansenist, he admits that the evidence in support of them was clear, complete, and without a flaw. But yet he rejects them, and that solely because of "the absolute impossibility, or miraculous nature of the events"! It behoves us to regard such evidence with suspicion; but to accept the evidence and yet to reject the facts thus established, is indeed "to destroy the very foundations of all human testimony."

4

ESSENTIAL VALUE OF MIRACLES

THAT Paley and those who follow him have mistaken and misstated the evidential value of the miracles of Christ may seem to some a startling proposition ; but it is by no means a novel one. To this error, moreover, it is that the argument against miracles in John Stuart Mill's " Essays on Religion" owes its seeming cogency.

The unbelief of the Christianised sceptic compares unfavourably with the agnosticism of the honest infidel. The one in rejecting miracles destroys the authenticity of the Gospels, and thus recklessly undermines the foundations of Christianity. The object of the other is a defence of human reason against supposed encroachments upon its authority. The one trades in sophistries which have been again and again refuted and exposed. The other propounds arguments which have never yet been adequately answered. The pseudo-Christian practically joins hands with the atheist ; for no amount of special pleading will avail to silence Paley's challenge, "Once believe there is a God, and miracles are not incredible." The avowed agnostic seizes upon Paley's gratuitous assertion that a revelation can only be made by miracles, and he sets himself to prove that miracles are wholly invalid for such a purpose.

Among English men of letters Mill's position is almost unique. From the account of his childhood in that saddest of books, his " Autobiography," it would appear that he approached the study of Christianity from the standpoint of a cultured pagan. He was wholly unconscious, therefore, that his argument against the theologian's position was entirely in accord with the teaching of Scripture. " A revelation cannot be proved Divine unless by external evidence " : such is his mode of restating Paley's thesis. And the problem this involves may be explained by the following illustration.

A stranger appears, say in London, the metropolis

of the world, claiming to be the bearer of a Divine revelation to mankind, and in order to accredit his message he proceeds to display miraculous power. Let us assume for the moment that after the strictest inquiry the reality of the miracles is established, and that all are agreed as to their genuineness. Here, then, we are face to face with the question in the most practical way. If the "Christian argument" be sound we are bound to accept whatever gospel this prophet proclaims. And no one who knows anything of human nature will doubt that it would be generally received. The Christian, however, would be kept back by the words of the inspired apostle: "But though we *or an angel from heaven* should preach unto you any gospel other than that which we preached unto you, let him be anathema." [1] In a word, the Christian would at once give up his "Paley" and fall back upon the position of the sceptic in the "Essays on Religion"! He would insist, moreover, on bringing the new miracle-accredited gospel to the test of Holy Writ, and finding it inconsistent with the gospel he had already received, he would

[1] Gal. i. 8 (R.V.).

reject it. That is to say, he would test the message, not by the miracles, but by a preceding revelation known to be Divine.

That Christ came to found a new religion, and that Christianity was received in the world on the authority of miracles—these are theses which command almost universal acceptance in Christendom. It may seem startling to maintain that both are alike erroneous, and that the Christian position has been seriously prejudiced by the error. And yet this is the conclusion which the preceding argument suggests, and to which full and careful inquiry will lead us. Is it not a fact that those in whose midst the miracles of Christ were wrought were the very people who crucified Him as a profane impostor? Is it not a fact that when challenged to work miracles in support of His Messianic claims He peremptorily refused?[1]

"However," says Bishop Butler, in summing up his argument on this subject, "the fact is allowed that Christianity was professed to be received into the world upon the belief of miracles," and "that is what the first converts would have alleged as

[1] Matt. xii. 38, 39, xvi. 1–4.

their reason for embracing it." Language cannot
be plainer. The "first converts," having witnessed
the miracles, reasoned out the matter, and con-
cluded that he who wrought them must be sent of
God; and thus became converts. But where is
the authority for such a statement? As a matter
of fact not one of the disciples is reported to have
attributed his faith to that ground.[1] The narrative of the first Passover of the ministry, which
may seem at first sight to refute this, is in fact
the clearest proof of it. Here are the words:
"Many believed on His name, beholding His
signs which He did. But Jesus *did not trust
Himself unto them*, for that He knew all men."[2]
That is to say, He refused to recognise any such
discipleship.

Then follows the story of Nicodemus, who was
one of the number of these miracle-made converts.
He had reasoned himself into discipleship, precisely as Butler supposes; but, as Dean Alford
expresses it,[3] he had to be taught that "it is not

---

[1] If any should quote the case of Simon Magus as an exception, they are welcome to their argument!

[2] John ii. 23, 24 (R.V.).   [3] Greek Test. Com., John iii

learning that is needed for the kingdom, but *life*, and life must begin by birth." Such is throughout the testimony of St. John. Entirely in harmony with it is the testimony of St. Peter, who shared with him the special privilege of witnessing that greatest of the miracles, the Transfiguration on the Holy Mount. "Being born again (he writes), not of corruptible seed, but of incorruptible, *by the Word of God*." [1]

Still more striking and significant is the case of St. Paul. As great a reasoner as Butler, and moreover a man of unswerving devotion to what he deemed to be the truth, the completed testimony of the ministry and miracles of Christ left him a bitter opponent and persecutor of Christianity. " I obtained mercy" is his own explanation of the change which took place in him. And again, "It pleased God, who . . . called me by His grace, to reveal His Son in me." Some may call such language mystical. To others, who are themselves what St. Paul till then had been, it may

[1] 1 Pet. i. 23. Still more definite are the Lord's words addressed to Peter in response to the confession of His Messiahship, " Blessed art thou, Simon Bar-Jonah ; for flesh and blood hath not revealed it unto thee, but My Father which is in heaven " (Matt. xvi. 17).

even seem offensive. But whatever its meaning, and however regarded, certain it is that it implies something wholly different from what Bishop Butler's words would indicate.[1]

But if the miracles were not intended to be a ground of faith in Christ, why, it will be asked, were they given at all? They had a twofold character and purpose. Just as a good man who is possessed of the means and the opportunity to relieve suffering is impelled to action by his very nature, so was it with our blessed Lord. When "the Word was made flesh and tabernacled among us," it was, if we may so speak with reverence, a matter of course that sickness and pain and even death should give way before Him. He "went about doing good and healing all that were oppressed of the devil *because God was with Him.*" The sceptics talk as though our Lord were represented as stopping in His teaching at intervals in order to work some miracle to silence unbelief. The idea is absolutely grotesque in its

---

[1] St. Paul's testimony gains in emphasis because of the vision on the Damascus road which, but for his explicit words, might lead us to call him a miracle-made disciple.

falseness. On the contrary we read such statements as this, that "He did not many mighty
works because of their unbelief."[1] As a matter
of fact, while there is not recorded a single
instance in the whole course of His ministry
where faith appealed to Him in vain—and this
it is which makes the inexorable reign of law
to-day so strange and overwhelming—neither is
there recorded a solitary instance where the
challenge of unbelief was rewarded by a miracle.
Every challenge of the kind was met by referring
the caviller to the Scriptures.

And this suggests the second great purpose
for which the miracles were given. With the
Jew politics and religion were inseparable. Every
hope of spiritual blessing rested on the coming
of Messiah. With that advent was connected
every promise of national independence and
prosperity. The pious few who constituted the
little band of His true disciples thought first and
most of the spiritual aspect of His mission. The
multitude thought only of deliverance from the
Roman yoke, and the restoration of the bygone

[1] Matt. xiii. 58.

glories of their kingdom. In the case of all alike His chief credentials were to be sought in the Scriptures which foretold His coming, and to these it was that His ultimate appeal was always made. "Ye are searching the Scriptures," He said to the Jews, "and these are they which bear witness of Me, and ye will not come to Me." [1] "If they hear not Moses and the prophets neither will they be persuaded though one rose from the dead." [2]

In this respect the evidence of the miracles was purely incidental. It is nowhere suggested that they were given to accredit the teaching; their evidential purpose was solely and altogether to accredit *the Teacher*. It was not merely that they were miracles, but that they were such miracles as the Jews were led by their Scriptures to expect. Their significance depended on their special character,[3] and their relation to a preceding revelation accepted as Divine by those for whose benefit they were accomplished.

---

[1] John v. 39, 40 (R.V.).   [2] Luke xvi. 31.

[3] Very strikingly is this exemplified in John the Baptist's case (Matt. xi. 2–5 ; see also John v. 36).

And this suggests, it may be remarked in passing, another flaw in the Christian argument from miracles, as usually stated. What is supernatural is not of necessity Divine. "Every one who works miracles is sent of God : this man works miracles, therefore He is sent of God." The logic of the syllogism is perfect. But the Jew would rightly repudiate the major premise, and of course reject the conclusion. As a matter of fact he attributed the miracles of Christ to Satan, and our Lord met the taunt, not by denying Satanic power, but by appealing to the nature and purpose of His acts. As they were manifestly aimed against the archenemy, they could not, He urged, be assigned to his agency.

The subordination of the testimony of miracles to that of Scripture appears more plainly still in the teaching after the resurrection. " Beginning (we read) at Moses and all the prophets He expounded unto them in all the Scriptures the things concerning Himself." And again, " These are the words which I spake unto you while I was yet with you, that all things must be fulfilled which were written in the law of Moses and in the prophets and in the Psalms concerning Me."[1] Nor was it otherwise when the apostles took up the testimony. St. Peter's appeal, addressed to the Jews of Jerusalem, was to "all the prophets, from Samuel and those that follow after, as many as have spoken."[2] Such also was St. Paul's defence when arraigned before Agrippa: "I continue unto this day (he declared) witnessing both to small and great, saying none other things than those which the prophets and Moses did say should come."[3] And when we turn to the dogmatic teaching of the Epistles we have the same truth still more explicitly enforced, that Christ "was *a minister of the circumcision* for the truth of God, to confirm the promises made unto the fathers, and that the Gentiles might glorify God for His mercy, *as it is written*."[4]

Page after page might thus be filled to prove the falseness of the dictum here under discussion. "A new religion!" It would be nearer the truth

---

[1] Luke xxiv. 27, 44. This threefold division of the Old Testament was the one commonly adopted by the Jew—the law, the prophets, and the "Hagiographa." The Psalms stood first in the third division, and thus came to give its name to the whole.

[2] Acts iii. 24.   [3] Acts xxvi. 22.   [4] Rom. xv. 8, 9.

to declare that one great purpose of Messiah's advent was to put an end to the reign of religion altogether. Such a statement would be entirely in keeping with the spirit of the only passage in the New Testament where the word occurs in relation to the Christian life.[1] Christ was Himself the reality of every type, the substance of every shadow, the fulfilment of every promise of the old religion. Whether we speak of the altar or the sacrifice, the priest or the temple in which He ministered, Christ was the antitype of all. His purpose was not to set these aside that He might set up others in their place—He came, not to destroy the law and the prophets, but to *fulfil* them. The very details of that elaborate ritual, the very furniture of that gorgeous shrine which was the scene and centre of the national worship, all pointed to Him. The ark of the covenant, the mercy-seat which covered it, the most holy place itself, and the veil which shut it in—all were but types of Him. The several altars and the many sacrifices bore witness to His infinite perfections and the varied aspects of His death as

[1] James i. 27.

bringing glory to God and full redemption to mankind. In plain truth, the attempt to set up a religion now, in the sense in which Judaism was a religion, is to deny Christianity and to apostatise from Christ.[1]

In the light of this truth the force of the sceptic's argument is wholly dissipated. When the Nazarene appeared, the question with the Jew was not whether, like another John the Baptist, He was "a man sent of God," but whether He was the Sent One, the Messiah to whom all their religion pointed and all their Scriptures bore testimony. "We have found the Messiah :" "We have found Him of whom Moses in the law, and the prophets, did write."[2] Such were the words in which His disciples gave expression to their faith, and by which they sought to draw others to Him. The question, then, is not whether a revelation can be accredited by external evidence, but whether such evidence can avail to accredit a person whose coming has been foretold. And this no accurate thinker would for a moment dispute.

[1] As regards the use of the word "Religion," see Appendix, Note II.   [2] John i. 41, 45.

In Dean Swift's fierce invective against the Irish bishops of his day he suggested that they were highwaymen who, having waylaid and robbed the prelates appointed by the Crown, had entered on their Sees in virtue of the stolen credentials. The whole point of this satire lay in the theoretical possibility of the suggestion. Nothing is more difficult in certain circumstances than to accredit an envoy. But, if he be expected, the merest trifle may suffice. An agent is sent upon some mission of secrecy and danger. A messenger will follow later with new and full instructions for his guidance. The messenger is described to him, but his sense of the peril of his position makes him plead that he shall have adequate credentials. In response to his appeal I pick up a scrap of paper, tear it in two, and handing him the half I tell him that the other moiety will be presented by the envoy. No document, however elaborate, would give surer proof of his identity than would that torn piece of paper.

Thus we see in what sense, and how certainly and simply, "external evidence" may avail "to accredit a revelation." And the sceptic's objection being set aside, he is again confronted with the irrefutable force of Paley's argument upon the main issue.

But another question claims notice here, ignored alike by exponent and objector. They have discussed the problem from the purely human standpoint, whereas the revelation offered for our acceptance claims to be Divine. Man is but a creature ; can God not speak to him in such wise that His word shall carry with it its own sanction and authority ? To assert that God *cannot* speak thus to man is practically to deny that He is God. To assert that He has never in fact spoken thus involves a transparent *petitio principii*. It might be urged that the authenticity of prophecy and promise has been established by their fulfilment. But certain it is that the prophets declare that God did thus speak to them, the Scriptures assume it, and the faith of the Christian endorses it.

5

A NEW DISPENSATION

IN the preceding chapter it has been shown that on this question of the evidential value of miracles the infidel is right and the Christian is wrong. It is not true that a revelation can only be made by miracles. The error of Paley's thesis can be demonstrated by argument. It can be exemplified moreover by reference to the case of the Baptist, who, though the bearer of a Divine revelation of supreme importance, had no miracles to appeal to in support of it.[1]

It has been further argued that, so far as their evidential force was concerned, the "Christian miracles" were for that favoured people "of whom, as concerning the flesh, Christ came." And if

[1] John x. 41.

this be well founded we shall be prepared to find that so long as the kingdom was being preached to Jews, miracles abounded, but that when the gospel appealed to the heathen world, miracles lost their prominence, and soon entirely ceased. The question remains whether the sacred record will confirm this supposition.

Who can fail to mark the contrast between the earlier and the later chapters of the Acts of the Apostles? Measured by years the period they embrace is comparatively brief; but morally the latter portion of the narrative seems to belong to a different age. And such is in fact the case. A new dispensation has begun, and the Book of the Acts covers historically the period of the transition. "To the Jew first" is stamped on every page of it. The Saviour's prayer upon the Cross [1] had secured for the favoured nation a respite from judgment. And the forgiveness asked for carried with it a right to priority in the proclamation of the great amnesty. When "the apostle of the circumcision," by express revelation, brought the gospel to Gentiles they were rele-

[1] Luke xxiii. 34.

gated to a position akin to that formerly held by the "proselytes of the gate."[1] And even "the apostle of the Gentiles" addressed himself first, in every place he visited, to the children of his own people. And this not from prejudice, but by Divine appointment. "*It was necessary*," he declared at Pisidian Antioch, "that the word of God should first be spoken to you."[2] Even at Rome, deeply though he longed to visit the Christians there,[3] his first care was to summon "the chief of the Jews," and to them "he testified the kingdom of God." And not until the testimony had been rejected by the favoured people did the word go forth, "The salvation of God is sent unto the Gentiles, and they will hear it."[4]

But, it will be objected, the Epistle to the Romans had been already written. True; but this only makes the narrative of the Acts still more significant. Those who profess to account for the Bible on natural principles seem ignorant of some of the main facts of the problem they

---

[1] Acts x. This is made still more clear by chap. xv. 2.

[2] Acts xiii. 46 (R.V.) ; *cf.* xvii. 2, 10, xviii. 1-4.

[3] Rom. i. 11.   [4] Acts xxviii. 17, 23, 28.

pretend to solve. They give no explanation of the *omissions* of Scripture. Contrast, for example, the first Gospel with the fourth. The writers of both shared the same teaching and were instructed in the same truths. How is it, then, that *Matthew* contains not a single sentence which is foreign to the purpose for which it was written, as presenting Israel's Messiah, the "son of David, the son of Abraham"?[1] How is it that *John*, which presents Him as the Son of God, omits even the record of his birth, and deals throughout with truth for all scenes and all time? And so with the Acts of the Apostles. As St. Paul's companion and fellow-labourer, the writer must have been familiar with the great truths revealed to the Church in the earlier Epistles, but not a trace of them appears in his treatise. Written under the Divine guidance for a definite purpose, nothing foreign to that purpose finds a place. To the superficial it may appear but a chance collection of incidents and memoirs, and yet, as has been rightly said,

[1] The prophetic utterance of Matt. xvi. 18 will not be deemed an exception to this.

"there is not a book upon earth in which the principle of intentional selection is more evident to a careful observer."[1]

The special and distinctive position enjoyed by the Jew was a main feature of the economy then about to close. "*There is no difference*"[2] is a canon of Christian doctrine. Men talk of the Divine history of the human race, but there is no such history. The Old Testament is the Divine history of *the family of Abraham.* The call of Abraham was chronologically the central point between the creation of Adam and the Cross of Christ, and yet the story of all the ages from Adam to Abraham is dismissed in eleven chapters. And if during the history of Israel the light of revelation rested for a time upon heathen nations, it was because the favoured nation was temporarily in captivity. But God took up the Hebrew race that they might be a centre and channel of blessing to the world. It was owing to their pride that they came to regard themselves as the only objects of Divine benevolence.

---

[1] The Bampton Lectures, 1864.   [2] Rom. iii. 22.

When some great French wine-grower appoints an agent in this country, he no longer supplies his wines except through that agent. His object, however, is not to hinder but to facilitate the sale, and to ensure that spurious wines shall not be palmed off upon the public in his name. Akin to this was the purpose with which Israel was called out in blessing. The knowledge of the true God was thus to be maintained on earth.[1] But the Jews perverted agency into a monopoly of Divine favour. That temple which was to have been a "house of prayer for all nations"[2] they treated as though it were not God's house, but their own, and ended by degrading it till it became at last "a den of thieves." But the position thus Divinely accorded them implied a *priority* in blessing. And this principle pervades not only the Old Testament Scriptures but the Gospels. To us indeed it is natural to read the Gospels in the light of the Epistles, and thus "to read into them" the wider truths

---

[1] Such was the spirit of their inspired Scriptures. See, *e.g.*, 2 Chron. vi. 32, 33; Psa. lxvii. 1–3, &c.

[2] Mark xi. 17 (R.V.).

of Christianity. But if the canon of Scripture ended with the Gospels this would be impossible.[1]

Suppose again the Epistles were there, but the Acts of the Apostles left out, how startling would appear the heading "To the Romans," which would confront us on turning from the study of the Evangelists! How could we account for the transition thus involved? How could we explain the great thesis of the Epistle, that there is no difference between Jew and Gentile, both being by nature on a common level of sin and ruin, both being called in grace to equal privi-

[1] "If," says the author of "Supernatural Religion," "Christianity consist of the doctrines preached in the Fourth Gospel, it is not too much to say that the Synoptics do not teach Christianity at all. The extraordinary phenomenon is presented of three Gospels, each professing to be complete in itself, and to convey the good tidings of salvation to man, which have actually omitted the doctrines which are the conditions of that salvation." This is a fair specimen of the sort of statement which, owing to prevailing ignorance of Holy Scripture, suffices to undermine the faith even of cultured people in our day. The Gospels were not written "to teach Christianity," but to reveal Christ in the different aspects of His person and work as Israel's Messiah, Jehovah's servant, Son of Man and Son of God. No one of them is "complete in itself"; and the Fourth alone expressly professes to teach the way of salvation (John xx. 31).

leges and glory? The earlier Scriptures will be searched in vain for teaching such as this. Not the Old Testament merely but even the Gospels themselves are seemingly separated from the Epistles by a gulf. To bridge over that gulf is the Divine purpose for which the Acts of the Apostles has been given to the Church. The earlier portion of the book is the completion of and sequel to the Gospels; its concluding narrative is introductory to the great revelation of Christianity.

But was not the death of Stephen, recorded in the seventh chapter, the crisis of the Pentecostal testimony? Undoubtedly it was; and thereupon "the apostle *to the Gentiles*" received his commission. But it was a crisis akin to that which marked the ministry of our blessed Lord Himself when the Council at Jerusalem decreed his destruction.[1] From that time He enjoined silence respecting His miracles,[2] and His teaching became veiled in parables.[3] But though His ministry entered upon this altered phase, it continued until

[1] Matt. xii. 14.   [2] Ibid. xii. 15, 16.
[3] Ibid. xiii.

His death. So was it in the record of the Acts. Progress in revelation, like growth in nature, is gradual, and sometimes can be appreciated only by its developments. The apostle to the circumcision gives place to the apostle to the Gentiles as the central figure in the narrative, but yet in every place the Jew is still accorded a priority in the offer of blessing, and it is not until, in every place from Jerusalem round to Rome, that blessing has been despised, that the Pentecostal dispensation is brought to a close by the promulgation of the solemn decree, "The salvation of God is sent unto the Gentiles."[1]

The hopes excited in the breasts of the disciples by their Lord's last words of cheer and promise were more than realised. Converts flocked to them by thousands, and "signs and wonders were wrought among the people." And, as already noticed, not only was Divine power in exercise to accredit their testimony, but also to deliver them from outrage, and rescue them from bonds and imprisonment. Nor was St. Paul behind the rest in these respects. But compare

[1] See Appendix, Note III.

the record of Pentecostal days with the narrative of his imprisonment in Rome, and mark the change! When dragged to gaol at Philippi as a common disturber of the peace, Heaven came down to earth in answer to his midnight prayer, the prison doors flew open, his gaoler became a disciple, and the magistrates who had committed him, besought him, with obsequious words, to comply with commands they no longer dared to enforce. But now he is "the prisoner of the Lord." His bonds are known everywhere to be for Christ.[1] In other words, there is no side issue, no incidental charge, as at Philippi, to conceal the true character of the accusation against him. It is a public fact that it is only because he is a teacher of Christianity that he is held in bonds. If the received theory respecting miracles be well founded, this is the scene and here is the occasion for "signs and wonders and mighty deeds," such as he had appealed to in his earlier career.[2] But Heaven is silent. There is no earthquake now to awe his persecutors. No angel messenger strikes off his

[1] Phil. i. 13.   [2] 2 Cor. xii. 12.

chains. He stands alone, forsaken of men, even
as his Master was, and seemingly forsaken of
God.[1] How natural the sceptic's taunt that
miracles were cheap with the peasants of Galilee
and the rabble of Jerusalem! A miracle at
Nero's Court might indeed have "accredited
Christianity." In truth, it might have shaken
the world. But miracle there was none; for,
the special testimony to the Jew having ceased,
the purpose for which miracles were given was
accomplished.

Like a day that breaks with unclouded splen-
dour, and approaches noontide in all the glory
of perfect summer, but then begins to wane,
and early closes in amidst the gloom of gather-
ing storm-clouds that shut out the sky and
darken all the scene, so was it with the course
of that brief story. At the first great Pentecost
three thousand converts were baptized in a single
day, the manifested power of God filled every
soul with awe, and those who were His own had
"gladness of heart" and "favour with all the

---

[1] 2 Tim. iv. 16. This passage disposes of the tradition that
St. Peter was Bishop of Rome.

people." And when the first threat of persecution drove them together in prayer, "the place was shaken where they were assembled . . . and with great power gave the apostles witness of the resurrection of the Lord Jesus."[1] The seeming check of the first martyr's death was followed by the conversion of him who caused it, the fierce persecutor and blasphemer, won over to the faith he had struggled to destroy, and chained to the chariot-wheels of the triumph of the gospel.[2] But now we see that same Paul, albeit the greatest of the apostles and the foremost champion the faith has ever known, standing alone at Cesar's judgment-seat, a weak, crushed man, given up to death to satisfy the policy or caprice of Imperial Rome.

In days to come "the song of Moses and the song of the Lamb" shall mingle once again in the anthem of the redeemed:[3] the song of Moses—

" I will sing unto the Lord for He hath triumphed gloriously,
The horse and his rider hath He thrown into the sea "—

that song of the public triumph of Divine power openly displayed ; and the song of the Lamb—

[1] Acts iv. 23-33.   [2] 2 Cor. ii. 14.   [3] Rev. xv. 3.

the song of that deeper but hidden triumph of faith in the unseen. But now the song of Moses has ceased, and the Church's only song is the song of Him who overcame, and won the throne through open defeat and shame. The days of the "rushing mighty wind," "the tongues of fire," the earthquake shock, are past. The anchor of the Christian's hope is firmly fixed in the veiled realities of heaven. He endures "as seeing Him who is invisible."

6

CHRISTIANITY DISTINGUISHED

THE Sovereign of the Universe is on the whole a good Sovereign, but with so much business on His hands that He has not time to look into details. Such was Cicero's apology two thousand years ago for Jupiter's neglect of his terrestrial kingdom.[1] And the words would fairly express the vague thoughts which float through the minds of common men if they think of God at all in relation to the affairs of earth. But there are times in every life when, in the language of the old Psalm, "heart and flesh cry out for the living God." [2] The *living* God: not a mere Providence, but a real Person—a God to help us as our fellow-man would help if only he had the power.

---

[1] Froude's " Cesar, a Sketch " p. 87.   [2] Psa. lxxxiv. 2.

And at such times men pray who never prayed before ; and men who are used to pray, pray with a passionate earnestness they never knew before. But what comes of it ? "When I cry and call for help He shutteth out my prayer":[1] such is the experience of thousands. Men do not speak of these things ; but, as they brood over them, the cold mist of a settled unbelief quenches the last spark of faith in hearts chilled by a sense of utter desolation, or roused to rebellion by a sense of wrong.

To some no doubt all this will savour of the mingled profanity and ignorance of unbelief. But by many these pages will be welcomed as giving full and fair expression to familiar thoughts. And the statement of these difficulties here is made with a view to their solution. But where is that solution to be found ? It is no novel experience with men that Heaven should be silent. But what is new and strange and startling is that the silence should be so absolute and so prolonged ; that, through all the changing vicissitudes of the Church's history for nearly two thousand years

[1] Lam. iii. 8 (R.V.).

that silence should have remained unbroken. This it is which tries faith, and hardens unfaith into open infidelity.

Can this mystery be solved? Mere speculations respecting it are profitless. The solution must be found in Holy Scripture, if at all. The Old Testament, of course, will throw no light on it. Neither will the Gospels afford a clew; for these are the record of "days of heaven upon earth." Nor yet need it be sought in the Acts of the Apostles, for, as already seen, the Book is the record of a transitory dispensation marked by abundant displays of the power of God among men. Is it not clear that if the key to the great secret of the Gentile dispensation can be found at all, it is in the writings of the apostle to the Gentiles that we must make search for it?

But here the ways divide. The wide and well-worn highway of religious controversy will never lead us to the truth we seek. *That* is reached only by a path which the general reader will refuse. Our choice lies between a study of these Epistles viewed as disclosing the "Pauline" developments, or perversions, of the teaching of the great Rabbi of Nazareth, or as containing that further revelation promised and foreshadowed by our Divine Lord in the later discourses of His ministry on earth. The one road is deemed the highway of modern enlightenment, the other is disparaged as a by-path now disused, or frequented only by the mystic and the unlearned. But in this sphere popularity is no test of truth. Let the atheistic evolutionist account for it if he can, the fact remains that man is essentially a religious being. He may sink so low as to deify humanity and make self his god, but a god of some sort he must have.[1] Religion is a necessity to him. The Christian religion prevails in Christendom ; other systems hold sway among the decaying civilisations of the world ; but neither the deepest degradation nor the highest enlightenment has ever produced a single nation or tribe of atheists.

This undoubted fact, however, may well give rise to most serious thoughts. It cannot be admitted

[1] "We know, and it is our pride to know, that man is by his constitution a religious animal ; that atheism is against, not only our reason but our instincts ; and that it cannot prevail long" (Edmund Burke). "Street arabs and advanced thinkers," is Mr. Balfour's classification of the exceptions to this rule ("Defence of Philosophic Doubt").

that the element of *truth* is of no account in religion, or that all these religions are equally acceptable. And once we come to the question of their relative excellence the religion of Christendom defies all comparison. May we, then, maintain that all adherents of the Christian religion are assured of Divine favour? Let us for a moment, forgetting what is due to "the spirit of the age," assume the Divine authority of Scripture, and we shall find ourselves confronted by doubts whether religion in this sense is of any avail whatever. Judaism was, indeed, a Divine religion. It had "ordinances of Divine service and its sanctuary,"[1] Divinely appointed in a sense to which no other system could pretend. And yet we read: "He is not a Jew who is one outwardly, neither is that circumcision which is outward in the flesh; but he is a Jew who is one inwardly, and circumcision is that of the heart."[2] And again, "For neither is circumcision anything, nor uncircumcision, but a new creature."[3] Now, if in a religion which seemed to consist so much in externals, the externals were absolutely of no value whatever save

[1] Heb. ix. 1 (R.V.).   [2] Rom. ii. 28   Gal. vi. 15.

as they had their counterpart and reality in a man's heart and life, this surely must be still more true of Christianity. May we not assert with confidence that he is not a *Christian* who is one outwardly, but he only is a Christian who is one inwardly? May we not maintain that there is a distinction sharp and clear between *Christianity* and the religion of Christendom.

In the case of the Roman and Greek Churches, this distinction becomes a deep and yawning gulf. And further, as Mr. Froude has well said, in those countries which rejected the Reformation, " culture and intelligence have ceased to interest themselves in a creed which they no longer believe. The laity are contemptuously indifferent, and leave the priests in possession of the field in which reasonable men have ceased to expect any good thing to grow. This is the only fruit of the Catholic reaction of the sixteenth century." And he adds : " If the same phenomena are beginning to be visible in England, coincident with the repudiation by some of the clergy of the principles of the Reformation ; and if they are permitted to carry through their Catholic 'revival,' the divorce between intelligence and Christianity will be as complete among ourselves as it is elsewhere."

"Between intelligence and *Christianity*" a divorce is impossible. But by " Christianity" the author here means " the religion of Christendom "; and with this correction his assertion is irrefutable. Mr. Balfour's "Foundations of Belief" escapes the difficulty here suggested by stopping short at the very threshold. His work is " *introductory* to the study of theology." And here his criticisms are searching, and his logic is without a flaw. But one step more would have brought him to the point where the ways divide. What is the theology he is aiming at? Is it the religion of Christendom — a human religion based on a Divine ideal, framed to reach and regulate men's opinions and conduct so far as the spiritual side of their complex being is concerned? Or is it *Christianity*—a Divine revelation commanding the faith and thus moulding the character and con- trolling the whole life of those who receive it?

In the estimation of some the great religion of Asia compares favourably with that of Christen- dom, on account of its freedom from priestcraft and ceremonial observances, its repudiation of penance and everything of mere asceticism, and the singular truth and beauty of its doctrine of "the middle path." But the comparison is altogether dishonest. It is drawn between the ideal Buddhism of our English admirers of Gautama, and the Christian system in its more corrupt developments. The practical Buddhism of Buddhist races is a gross and degrading superstition, and it cannot compare with the Christian religion even at its worst. And even the refined Buddhism presented by its Western exponents is wanting in that ennobling element which is distinctive of Christianity. The wholly legendary and half mythical story of Gautama's life are a poor equivalent for the well-ascertained facts of the ministry of Christ.[1] Here let a witness speak whose judgment is warped by no religious bias.

[1] For a calm, scholarly, and crushing refutation of those who, like de Bunsen, Seydel, &c., represent Buddhism as the original of Christianity, and of those who, like Sir Edwin Arnold, read Christianity into Buddhism, see Prof. Kellogg's "Light of Asia and Light of the World" (Macmillan).

The Buddhism of Gautama, I may add, has no claim to be reckoned a *religion*, for it has no God. It was not a religion at all, but merely a philosophy. But his followers, in obedience to the instinctive craving of human nature for a religion, made Gautama

"It was reserved for Christianity," says Mr. Lecky, "to present to the world an ideal character which, through all the changes of eighteen centuries has filled the hearts of men with an impassioned love, has shown itself capable of acting on all ages, nations, temperaments, and conditions ; has not only been the highest pattern of virtue, but the highest incentive to its practice, and has exerted so deep an influence that it may be truly said that the simple record of three short years of active life has done more to regenerate and soften mankind than all the disquisitions of philosophers and all the exhortations of moralists. This has, indeed, been the well-spring of whatever has been best and purest in the Christian life. Amid all the sins and failings, amid all the priestcraft, the persecutions, and fanaticism which have defaced the Church, it has preserved in the character and example of its Founder an enduring principle of regeneration."

If the Christian religion, even in its outward and

himself their God. And the Buddhism of later times has invariably assimilated some of the elements of the base polytheisms by which it has been surrounded.

human side, can justly claim such a testimony as this, what words are adequate to describe CHRISTIANITY in the higher and deeper sense? And let no one carp at this distinction as fanciful or forced. In fact, it is broad and vital. Just as the religion of Asia is based on the life and teaching of Gautama, so the religion of Christendom, regarded as a human system, claims to be based on the life and teaching of the great Rabbi of Nazareth. But the advent and ministry of Christ were, in fact, *introductory* to the great revelation of Christianity. Thus was crowned and completed, as it were, the fabric which had been rearing for ages. In the public aspect of it His mission had relation to the economy about to close. He was "born under the law." [1] He "was a minister of the *circumcision* for the truth of God." Hence His words, "I am not sent but unto the lost sheep of the house of Israel." And as the result, infinite love, and grace which knows no distinctions, were restrained. "I have a baptism to be baptized with," He exclaimed, "and how am I straitened till it be accomplished!"

[1] Gal. iv. 4.

7

ANOTHER GREAT TRUTH

JUST half a century ago the theologians of Christendom were startled by the publication of Ferdinand Christian Baur's treatise on Paul. It was an epoch-making book. The author's critical researches had led him to assert the unquestionable authenticity of the Epistles to the Romans, the Corinthians, and the Galatians. And fastening on these writings as our safest guides in historical inquiries respecting the character and rise of primitive Christianity, he went on to demonstrate its Pauline origin. "These authentic documents," he urged (to quote a recent writer), "reveal antitheses of thought, a Petrine and a Pauline party in the Apostolic Church. The Petrine was the primitive Christian, made up of men who, while believing in Jesus as the Messiah, did not cease to be Jews, whose Christianity was but a narrow neo-Judaism. The Pauline was a reformed and Gentile Christianity, which aimed at universalising the faith in Jesus by freeing it from the Jewish law and traditions. The universalism of Christianity, and, therefore, its historical importance and achievements, are thus really the work of the Apostle Paul. His work he accomplished not with the approval and consent, but against the will and in spite of the efforts and oppositions, of the older apostles, and especially of their more inveterate adherents who claimed to be the party of Christ." [1]

If we are to understand the sequel to the present argument we must rescue from its false environment of German rationalism the important truth which Baur thus brought to light and distorted.[2] We must needs recognise the intensely Jewish character of the Pentecostal dispensation. And in

[1] "The Place of Christ in Modern Theology," by Principal Fairbairn, D.D., p. 267.

[2] A dozen years before Baur's "Paul" appeared, the truth thus attributed to him was discussed at the then celebrated "Powerscourt meetings" in Ireland !

this connection we must also apprehend the two-fold aspect of the death of Christ. The Cross was the manifestation of Divine love without reserve or limit; but it was also the expression of man's unutterable malignity. Did reverence permit us to give play to imagination on such a subject, we might suppose the death of Christ accomplished by the Roman power in spite of protests and appeals from an aggrieved and down-trodden Jewish people. More than this, we might suppose "the King of the Jews" given up to death on grounds of public policy, yet treated to the last with all the respect and homage due to His personal character and royal claims.

And who will dare to aver that the atoning efficacy of the death of our Divine Lord, how-ever accomplished, could be less than infinite? But mark the emphasis which Scripture lays upon the *manner* of His death. It was "the death of *the Cross*." No element of contempt or hate was wanting. Imperial Rome decreed it, but it was the favoured people who demanded it. The "wicked hands" by which they murdered their Messiah were those of their heathen masters, but the responsibility for the act was all their own. Nor was it the ignorant rabble of Jerusalem that forced the Roman government to set up the cross on Calvary. Behind the mob was the great Council of the nation. Neither was it a sudden burst of passion that led these men to clamour for His death. Hostile sects forgot their differences in deep-laid plots to compass His destruction. The time, moreover, was the Paschal feast, when Jews from every land were gathered in Jerusalem. Every interest, every class, every section of that people shared in the great crime. Never was there a clearer case of *national* guilt. Never was there an **act** for which *a nation* could more justly be summoned to account.

But Infinite mercy could forgive even that transcendent sin, and in Jerusalem itself it was that the great amnesty was first proclaimed. Pardon and peace were preached, by Divine command, to the very men who crucified the Son of God ! But here prevailing misconceptions are so fixed that the whole significance of the narrative is lost. The apostles were Divinely guided to declare that if, even then, the " men of Israel" repented, their Messiah would return to fulfil to them all that their own prophets had foretold and promised of spiritual and national blessing.[1]

To represent this as *Christian* doctrine, or the institution of "a new religion," is to betray ignorance alike of Judaism and of Christianity The speakers were Jews—the apostles of One who was Himself "a minister of the circumcision." Their hearers were Jews, and as Jews they were addressed. The Pentecostal Church which was based upon the testimony was intensely and altogether Jewish. It was not merely that the converts were Jews, and none but Jews,

---

[1] Though the Revisers have reproduced St. Peter's words in one important passage which the Authorised Version has misread, yet to take these simple words in their plain and obvious meaning is to risk being looked upon as either fool or faddist. The words are: "Repent ye therefore, and turn again, that your sins may be blotted out, that so there may come seasons of refreshing from the presence of the Lord; and that He may send the Christ who hath been appointed for you, even Jesus; whom the heaven must receive until the times of restoration of all things, whereof God spake by the mouth of His holy prophets. . . . Ye are the sons of the prophets and of the covenant which God made with your fathers" (Acts iii. 19, &c.). The whole passage should be carefully studied, and by all means see Alford's notes, showing how fully and definitely all this refers to Jewish hopes and promises.

but that the idea of evangelising Gentiles never was even mooted. When the first great persecution scattered the disciples, and they "went everywhere preaching the Word," they preached, we are expressly told, "to none but to the Jews." [1] And when after the lapse of years Peter entered a Gentile house, he was publicly called to account for conduct that seemed so strange and wrong.[2]

In a word, if "To the Jew first" is characteristic of the Acts of the Apostles as a whole, "To the Jew only" is plainly stamped upon every part of these early chapters, described by theologians as the "Hebraic section" of the book. The fact is clear as light. And if any are prepared to account for it by Jewish prejudice and ignorance, they may at once throw down this volume, for it is here assumed that the

[1] Acts viii. 1, 4 ; *q.* xi. 19. It is noteworthy that at this time all the believers went out preaching *except the apostles.* And yet there are those who maintain that preaching is an exclusively apostolic function !

[2] Acts xi. The words "they that were of the circumcision" might seem to suggest that there were Gentiles at that time in the Church. But, as Dean Alford says, Luke uses the phrase from the standpoint of the time when he was writing : "In this case *all* those spoken of would belong to the circumcision."

apostles of the Lord, speaking and acting in the memorable days of Pentecostal power, were Divinely guided in their work and testimony.

The Jerusalem Church, then, was Jewish. Their Bible was the Jewish Scriptures. The Jewish temple was their house of prayer and common meeting-place.[1] Their beliefs and hopes and words and acts all marked them out as Jews. Hence the amazing number of the converts. On the day of Pentecost alone three thousand were baptized.[2] Soon afterwards their company would seem to have more than trebled.[3] At the time of the sin and death of Ananias and Sapphira, still further " multitudes, both of men and women," were added to their company. And at the time of the appointment of the men who, by a strange vagary of tradition, have been misnamed " the deacons," [4] it is recorded that

---

[1] Acts ii. 46, iii. 1, v. 42. [2] Ibid. ii. 41.

[3] Ibid. iv. 4. If " the number of the *men* came to be about five thousand," it is reasonably certain that the whole company was double this number at least.

[4] They are never so called in the Acts. Indeed, our English word " deacon " has no equivalent in ancient or in Biblical Greek, and if the Revisers had been true to their avowed principles of translation the word would have disappeared. Διάκονος is used

"the number of the disciples multiplied in Jerusalem greatly, and a great company of the priests were obedient to the faith." [1]   Nothing was further from the thoughts of these men than "founding a new religion." On the contrary, while hailing the rejected Nazarene as their national Messiah, they clung with passionate devotion to the religion of their fathers.

But what bearing has all this upon the question here? The Jews had crucified the Messiah. But now, when vengeance swift and terrible might have been expected to fall upon that guilty people, Divine mercy held back the judgment and called them once again to repentance. The testimony was full and clear, and it was confirmed by a signal display of miraculous power. But what was the answer of the men who sat "in Moses' seat"—the accredited leaders and representatives of the

twenty-two times in the Epistles, and should be rendered "minister" in every case, and especially in Phil. i. 1, and 1 Tim. iii. 8 and 12, where ministers are distinguished from bishops. In the Gospels it occurs eight times, and always as equivalent to "servant" in the common acceptation, save in John xii. 26, where it is used in a higher sense.

[1] Acts vi. 7.

nation?[1] By the murder of Stephen they re-enacted, so far as it was in their power to re-enact, the supreme tragedy of Calvary. Having regard to all the events which marked the interval, that further crime betokened a more deliberate hate, and therefore a greater depth of guilt, even than the Crucifixion itself. There was no popular clamour now to blind their judgment. When, some months before, in a formal meeting of their national senate, the plot to murder the apostles was first mooted, it was one of the great doctors of the Sanhedrin who intervened on their behalf.[2] Gamaliel's words, moreover, and the action which the council took on them, give proof how entirely the position and teaching of the apostles were within the scope of Jewish beliefs and hopes, and how thoroughly they were regarded as a Jewish sect.[3] But these men

[1] Matt. xxiii. 2.

[2] Acts v. 21, 33–40. I use the word murder advisedly, for under the Roman law the Jews had no power to put any one to death. See John xviii. 31. The crucifixion was a *judicial* murder; the stoning of Stephen was murder pure and simple.

[3] Acts v. 34–40; *cf.* xxii. 3. A quarter of a century later they were still known as "the sect of the Nazarenes" (Acts xxiv. 5). See p. 85 *post.*

were so blinded by religious rancour that no voice, human or Divine, could avail to restrain them.

Heaven's best gifts, when perverted or abused, often turn to what is virulently bad ; and religion, when divorced from spiritual life, appears to have some mysterious power to narrow and harden and deprave the human heart. "It cannot be that a prophet perish out of Jerusalem!"[1] The pathos of the words does not conceal their scathing irony. Among common men, however evil or degraded, a prophet might pass unharmed : *religious* men alone would persecute and murder him! In every age, indeed, religion has been the most implacable enemy of God, the most relentless persecutor of His people. Witness the tombs of the prophets! Witness the blood-stained pages of the Church's history! The Christian martyrs in unnumbered millions—for though their names are written in heaven, earth has kept no record of them — the best and purest and noblest of mankind, have been tortured and done to death in the name

[1] Luke xiii. 33.

of *religion.*[1] How just is the infidel's taunt that it radically vitiates the standard of human morals ! [2]

The men by whose hands the " first martyr " died were the very men who had been " the betrayers and murderers" of Christ. In times of riot or excitement mobs will commit excesses which, in his better moments, every man of them would deprecate. But these men were not of the class that mobs are made of. The high priest presided. Around him were the elders and the scribes. By the great Council of the nation it was that the deed was done. Its members were the acknowledged religious leaders of the people. Many of them, like Saul of Tarsus, himself the formal witness of the death, were men of blameless life, of untiring zeal and intensest piety. And as the cruel stones were

---

[1] The victims of the so-called Christian persecutions have been wildly estimated at over fifty millions ! Of the victims of *pagan* Rome I have never seen any estimate. And pagan persecutions also were in the name of religion ! From the death of Abel in primeval times down to the massacres of Armenian Christians to-day, religion has heaped up the tale of human guilt and sorrow.

[2] Mill's " Autobiography," p. 40.

showered upon that face which had shone like an angel's as they looked on it, it was hatred to the Nazarene that fired their hearts. Their King they had driven out: Stephen was the messenger sent after Him to declare anew their deliberate purpose to reject Him.[1] This was their answer to the heaven-sent testimony of Pentecost. "All manner of sin" against the Son might be forgiven; they had now committed that deeper sin against the Holy Ghost, for which there could be no forgiveness.[2]

During the forty years of Jeremiah's ministry the first destruction of Jerusalem was delayed. So now well-nigh forty years elapsed before the crash of that still more awful judgment which engulfed them. God is very pitiful, and then, as now, "He had compassion on His people and on His dwelling-place. But they mocked the messengers of God, and despised His words, and misused His prophets, until the wrath of the Lord arose against His people till there was no remedy."[3] But though the public event

---

[1] Luke xix. 14. [2] Matt. xii. 31, 32.
[3] 2 Chron. xxxvi. 15, &c.

which marked their fall was thus deferred, the death of Stephen was the secret crisis of their destiny. Never again was a public miracle witnessed in Jerusalem. The special Pentecostal proclamation [1] was withdrawn. The Pentecostal Church was scattered. The apostle of the Gentiles forthwith received his commission, and the current of events set steadily, and with continually increasing force, toward the open rejection of the long-favoured people and the public proclamation of the great characteristic truth of Christianity. Within that truth lies concealed the key to the mystery of a silent Heaven.

[1] Acts iii. 19–26.

8

ATTACKS REBUFFED

WE have now reached a stage in this inquiry where a retrospect may be opportune. Expression has been given to difficulties and doubts to which no thoughtful person is a stranger. And these, it has been seen, are rather intensified, than answered or removed, by an appeal to the mere surface current of Scripture testimony. The "Christian argument" from miracles has been shown to be not only inadequate, but faulty. And we have turned to the Acts of the Apostles to find how fallacious is the popular belief that the Jerusalem Church was *Christian*. In fact, it was thoroughly and altogether Jewish. The only difference, indeed, between the position of the disciples during the

"Hebraic period" of the Acts, and during the period of the Lord's earthly ministry, was that the great fact of the Resurrection became the burden of their testimony. And finally we have seen how the rejection of that testimony by the favoured nation led to the unfolding of the Divine purpose to deprive the Jew of his vantage-ground of privilege and to usher in the Christian dispensation.

The Divine religion of Judaism in every part of it, both in the spirit and the letter, pointed to the coming of a promised Messiah ; and to maintain that a man ceased to be a Jew because he cherished that hope, and accepted the Messiah when He came—this is a position absolutely grotesque in its absurdity. It would not be one whit more monstrous to declare that in our own day a man ceases to be a Christian if and when faith in Christ, from being a mere shibboleth of his creed, becomes a reality in his heart and life.

Twenty years after the Pentecostal Church was formed, the disciples were still regarded by their own nation as a Jewish sect. "The sect of the Nazarenes," Tertullus called them in his arraign-

ment of Paul before Felix; and Paul, in his
defence, repudiated the charge, claiming that the
followers of the Way were the true worshippers of
the ancestral God of his nation.[1] Israel fell, not
because the disciples, alive to the spiritual
significance of their religion, accepted Christ, but
because the nation rejected Him, and persisted in
that rejection, "despising His words and misusing
His prophets, till there was no remedy."

It would be an idle and profitless speculation
to discuss what would have been the course of
the dispensation if the Pentecostal testimony
had led the Jews to repentance. What concerns
us is the fact that Israel's fall was due to the
national rejection of Messiah, and that that fall
was "the reconciling of the world"[2]—a radical
change in God's attitude toward men, such as
the Old Testament Scriptures gave no indica-

---

[1] Acts xxiv. 5, 14. "After the Way, which they call a sect, so
serve I the God of our fathers" (see also xxviii. 22), and he goes on
to appeal to the law and the prophets. "The Way" came to be
the common expression for their teaching (see, *e.g.*, Acts xix. 9,
23, xxii. 4, xxiv. 14, 22 R.V.). And speaking before a heathen
judge he purposely uses, not the Jewish expression, ὁ θεὸς τῶν
πατέρων ἡμῶν, but the term familiar to the heathen, ὁ πατρῷος
θεός, the ancestral or tutelary God.

[2] Rom. xi. 15.

tion of, and even the Gospels foreshadowed but vaguely. We thus steer our course unswayed by the ignorance of the Christian sceptic and the animus of the avowed unbeliever. The one, disparaging the Epistles, turns back to the Sermon on the Mount to seek there an ideal Christianity: the other has no difficulty in showing that the teaching of Christ, when so perverted, is the dream of a visionary. The Sermon on the Mount combines principles of limitless scope with precepts designed for the time at which they were spoken, and the spiritually intelligent cannot fail to discriminate between the two. It was for such the Bible was written, and neither for infidels nor fools.[1]

We conclude, then, as we study the records of the Pentecostal Jewish Church, that the characteristic truths of Christianity have yet to be revealed. Turning back to the earlier Scriptures with the knowledge we now possess, we may find them there in embryo, but the full and formal promulgation of them must be sought in the Epistles. But here the parting of the ways will

[1] See Appendix, Note IV.

become still more definitely marked. In passing away from the ministry of "the apostle to the circumcision," we leave behind us, of course, the religion of Christendom—for is not St. Peter its patron saint? Mere Protestantism, moreover, has but little sympathy with studies of this kind. And as for that school of religious thought which seems for the moment to stand highest in the popular favour, we break with it entirely on entering upon the inquiry which lies before us. None such will accompany the truth-seeker as he passes on his lonely way.

But while other schools will be simply indifferent to this inquiry, open hostility will be the attitude of those who claim to be the party of progress and enlightenment. It may be well, therefore, to turn aside once again to examine their pretensions. No generous mind would willingly insult a man's religion, whether he be Christian or Jew, Mahometan or Buddhist. But when "religious" men pose as sceptics and critics, they come out into the open, and forfeit all "right of sanctuary.' Courtesy is due to the religious man who stands behind the *labarum* of his creed. Courtesy is no less due to the agnostic who refuses faith in all that lies outside the sphere of sense or demonstration. But what shall be said for those who discard belief in the supernatural while they claim to be the true exponents of a system which has the supernatural as its only basis ; or who deprecate belief in the inspiration of the Scriptures, while they profess to hold and teach that to which, apart from inspiration in the strictest sense, none but the credulous would listen ?

These men pretend to mental superiority ; but we only need to tear away the lion's skin they masquerade in to find—exactly what we might expect ! Here is a dilemma from which there is no escape. If the New Testament be Divinely inspired, we accept its teaching ; we believe that Jesus was the Son of God, that He was born of a virgin, that He died and rose again, that He ascended to heaven, and now sits as man at the right hand of God ; in a word, we are Christians, and to take any other position is to stultify ourselves by dethroning reason itself. If, on the other hand, the New Testament be not inspired, no consensus of mere human opinion or testimony, however ancient or venerable or widespread, would warrant our accepting figments so essentially incredible ; in a word, we are agnostics, and to take any other position is to pose as superstitious fools who would believe anything.

The Christian and the infidel cannot both be right, yet both are entitled to respect, for the one position is logically as unassailable as the other. But what shall be said for the unbelieving Christian, or the Christianised infidel ? If he be dishonest he is almost bad enough for a gaol ; if he be honest he is almost weak enough for an asylum. The weak deserve our pity ; the wicked our contempt. And their claim to be freethinkers, their affectation of intellectual superiority, give proof that with the majority the more generous alternative is the true one. The old Jewish proverb about straining out a gnat and swallowing a camel well describes their attempt to combine the most fastidious scepticism with the blindest faith. These modern Sadducees talk "as though wisdom were born with them " ; whereas, in fact, like their prototypes of old, they are the stupid advocates of an impossible compromise.

Let there be no misunderstanding here. It is not a question of demanding faith on grounds which are either false or inadequate. It is not a question of trading on the superstitious element in human nature, lest common men, in throwing off the restraints of religion, should allow liberty to degenerate into licence. This appeal is addressed to the fair-minded, the intelligent, the thoughtful. If we possess a revelation, and if the doctrines of Christianity are Divinely accredited as true, reason commands our acceptance of them, and unbelief is an outrage upon reason itself. If, on the other hand, we have no revelation ; or, what comes to the same thing, if the Divine element in Scripture is merely traditional, and must be separated from abounding error—picked out like treasure from a dust-heap—then we must either give up our Protestantism and fall back on the authority of the Church, or else we must needs face the matter fairly, and accept and act upon the dictum that "the rational attitude of the thinking mind towards the supernatural is that of scepticism." The superstitious will take refuge in the former alternative ; the latter will commend itself to all free and fearless thinkers. The former, indeed, is not only intellectually deplorable, but logically absurd. We are called upon to believe the Scriptures because the Church accredits them. The Bible is not infallible, but the Church is infallible, and upon the authority of the Church our faith can find a sure foundation.[1] But how do we know that the Church is to be trusted? The ready answer is, We know it upon the authority of the Bible. That is to say, we trust the Bible on the authority of the Church, and we trust the Church on the authority of the Bible! It is a bad case of "the confidence trick."

But, it will be said, is it not to the Church that we owe the Bible?[2] Regarded as a *book* we owe it indeed in a sense to the Church, just as we owe it to the printer. But in a sense which appeals to us more closely here in England we owe it to noble men who rescued it for us in defiance of the Church. Let not the Protestants of England forget William Tyndale. His life-

[1] This is the position assumed by "Lux Mundi." See specially pp. 340–341.

[2] The Old Testament we owe, of course, entirely to the Jews.

work was to bring the Bible within reach even of the humblest peasant. And for no other offence than this the Church hounded him to his death, never resting till it strangled him at the stake and flung his body to the flames.

But the Bible is more than a book—it is a *revelation;* and thus regarded, it is above the Church. We do not judge the Bible by the Church; we judge the Church and its teaching by the Bible.[1] This is our safeguard against the ignorance and tyranny of priestcraft. But in our day those who deprecate most strongly the tyranny of the priest are precisely those who champion

[1] The Church of England teaches unequivocally that there is neither salvation nor infallibility in the Church, and that the Church's authority in matters of faith is controlled and limited by Holy Writ (see Articles xviii.–xxi.). And this is Protestantism ; not a repudiation of authority in the spiritual sphere, but a revolt against the bondage of mere human authority falsely claiming to be Divine. It delivers us from the authority of " the Church," that we may be free to bow to the authority of God. " The Church " claims to mediate between God and man. But Christianity teaches that all pretensions of the kind are both false and profane, and points to our Divine Lord as the only Mediator. Protestantism is not our religion, but it leaves us with a free conscience and an open Bible, face to face with God. It is not an anchorage for faith ; but it is like the breakwater which renders our anchorage secure. It shields us from influences which make Christianity impossible.

most loudly the tyranny of the professor and the pundit. The occupant of a University chair cannot fail to be eminent in the branch of knowledge in which he excels, and his value as a specialist is unquestionable. But he may be so utterly unspiritual, and withal so deficient in judgment and common sense, that his opinion may be worth less than that of an intelligent peasant or a Christian schoolboy. The fabric of the Bible, he tells us, is wholly unreliable, but some of its most unbelievable mysteries are truths Divinely revealed. But what claim has he to be listened to in such a case? The setting of the trinket is worthless, and most of its seeming gems are spurious, but here and there he indicates a diamond or a pearl. But the profoundest knowledge of mathematics or Oriental dialects does not qualify a man to judge of pearls and diamonds. Still less does it fit him to recognise spiritual truths.[1]

If the Bible has really been discredited by modern research, let us have the honesty to own

[1] These men declare that to them our faith in Holy Writ seems foolishness. But Holy Writ warns us that "the natural man receiveth not the things of the Spirit of God : *for they are foolishness unto him*" (1 Cor. ii. 14).

the fact and the manliness to face its consequences. But if the Bible has not been thus discredited, if the results of modern research have been entirely in its favour,[1] then let us show a bolder front in our stand for faith. And let faith and unbelief measure their distance once again.

The Bible was written for honest hearts. It is addressed, moreover, to *spiritual* men. And what is the practical test of spirituality? "If any man think himself to be a prophet, or spiritual, let him acknowledge that the things which I write unto you are the commandments of the Lord":[2] these words betoken, not the insolence of a priest, but the authority of an inspired apostle. It is as believers then, and in the spirit of faith, that we turn to the Epistles.

[1] To record the points on which the Bible was formerly attacked, marking off those which modern research has disposed of—this is a task which awaits a competent pen. And when the book is written it will astonish both friends and foes.

[2] I Cor. xiv. 37.

9

CHRISTIAN DOCTRINE

" IN Christ's grand and simple creed, expressed in His plainest words, eternal life was the assured inheritance of those who loved God with all their hearts, who loved their neighbours as themselves, and who walked purely, humbly, and beneficently while on earth. In the Christian sects and churches of to-day, in their recognised formularies and elaborate creeds, all this is repudiated as infantine and obsolete ; the official means and purchase-money of salvation are altogether changed ; eternal life is reserved for those, and for those only, who accept, or profess, a string of metaphysical propositions conceived in a scholastic brain and put into scholastic phraseology " [1]

To any one who aims at having clear thoughts and well-based beliefs nothing is more helpful than

[1] W. R. Greg's " Creed of Christendom."

adverse criticism. Hence the value of the words here quoted. They may be taken, moreover, as expressing the opinions of a large and important class by whom the writer, though no longer with us, may still be claimed as a champion and representative.

A preliminary question which presents itself is, Where are we to find this "grand and simple creed" thus commended to our acceptance? If, as the agnostic tells us, the Gospels are mere human records, what can be sillier than to appeal to them for the teaching of Christ! It was a conceit of ancient writers to put long speeches into the mouths of their heroes, and the discourses attributed to the Nazarene fall at once into the category of romance. But we are told that while the evangelists are not to be trusted when they record plain events of which they were eye-witnesses, like the miracles of Christ, they are to be believed implicitly when they profess to record *verbatim* His prolonged discourses! If the Gospels be Divinely inspired, agnosticism is sheer folly: if they be not inspired, our faith is sheer superstition.

The next thought which these words suggest is that if eternal life be indeed reserved for those whose character and conduct are marked by absolute perfection, the whole human race is doomed.   Perfect love to God and man is a standard which excludes even the saintliest of saints, and common men may at once dismiss all hope of reaching it.   And yet the author is right. It is thus and only thus that eternal life can be *inherited* by any child of Adam.   What concerns us, then, is to inquire whether possibly some other road to blessing may be open to us.   *Agnosticism* is Greek for ignorance ; may we not hope that this particular agnostic is true to his name, and that Divine love goes far beyond what he seems ever to have realised or heard of ?

The statements here challenged are important as showing how seriously the great truth of the Reformation is prejudiced by the very prominence assigned to it in our Protestant system of theology. That it should loom great in our estimation is but natural, having regard to the fierceness of the struggle to which we owe its recovery.   And yet the dogma that justification is *by faith* is but a secondary truth, and ancillary to another of wider range and more transcendent moment. "For this cause it is on the principle of faith, that it may be according to Grace."[1] GRACE is the characteristic truth of Christianity. According to the great doctrinal treatise of the New Testament, we are "justified by grace," "justified by faith," "justified by blood"—that is, by the death of Christ in its application to us, for such is the meaning of the sacrificial figure of which the word "blood" is the expression in the New Testament. Grace is the principle on which God justifies a sinner; faith is the principle on which the benefit is received; and the death of Christ is the ground on which alone all this is possible—we are "justified freely by His grace through the redemption that is in Christ Jesus."[2]

And they who are thus justified can urge no claim to the benefit on the ground either of merit or of promise. For if we could earn a title to it, there were no need of redemption; and if

---

[1] Διὰ τοῦτο ἐκ πίστεως ἵνα κατὰ χάριν (Rom. iv. 16). Theology has no better definition of grace than that given by Aristotle (Rhet ii. 7).

[2] Rom. iii. 24.

God had pledged Himself by covenant to grant it, there were no room for grace. Grace is sovereign, but it is free.

There are two alternative principles on which alone justification is now theoretically possible. The one is by man's deserving it ; the other is through God's unmerited favour. Let a man, from the cradle to the grave, be everything he ought to be, and do everything he ought to do ; let him, as our author puts it, love God with all his heart, and his neighbour as himself, walking " purely, humbly, and beneficently while on earth," and such an one will " *inherit* eternal life." But all such pretensions betoken moral and spiritual ignorance and degradation. All men are *sinners ;* and being sinners they are absolutely dependent upon grace.

Mr. Greg's words are based on the incident in our Lord's ministry which called forth the parable of " The Good Samaritan." " A certain lawyer," desirous of testing the Saviour's doctrine, put to Him the question, " Master, what shall I do to inherit eternal life? " He had heard no doubt that the great Rabbi was heretical, disparaging the law of Moses, and pointing the common folk to an easy bypath to life. How great then must have been his surprise when he got answer, "What is written in the law? How readest thou?" In response he repeated the well-known words, so familiar to every Jew, enjoining love to God and man. And surprise must have grown into astonishment when the Saviour added, "Thou hast answered right; this do and thou shalt live." The strictest legalist in the Sanhedrin could find no flaw in teaching such as that! But the question was, how a man could *inherit* life, and to such a question, one and only one answer was possible. To hide his confusion the lawyer at once proposed a further question, "And who is my neighbour?" thus seeking to escape upon a side issue, as is the way with lawyers of every age. And this drew from the Lord that exquisite story which has taken such hold upon the minds of men. The Greek word for "neighbour" is the *one near*, and the lawyer's inquiry implied that he was not bound to love *every one* with whom he came in contact. The high-caste Jew, if such a phrase may be allowed, would rather die than owe his rescue to a Samaritan, so the Lord brings a Samaritan into the parable, contrasts his conduct with that of the Levite and the priest, and asks which of the three acted as neighbour to the poor wretch whom the robbers had left half dead upon the roadside.

Such was the surface teaching of the parable, but in common with every other parable, it had a hidden and spiritual meaning. He had answered the inquiry how a perfect being could *inherit* life : He now unfolds how a ruined sinner can be saved. The traveller upon the road from the city of blessing to the city of the curse is robbed of his all, and left wounded almost to death, and helpless. A priest and a Levite pass by. Why a priest and a Levite ? Because He would thus impersonate the law and, in a word, religion. These could help a man who was able to help himself, but for the helpless sinner they can do nothing. "But a certain Samaritan came where he was." Why a Samaritan ? Because He would teach that the Saviour is One whom, but for his ruin and misery, the sinner would despise and repel. "And"—let us mark the words—"when he saw him he had compassion on him, and went to him, and bound up his wounds, and set him on his own beast, and brought him to an inn, and took care of him ; " and at the inn he paid the reckoning, and made provision for his future.

In every detail the story has its counterpart in spiritual truth. It tells of a Saviour who *saves ;* who comes to a sinner where he is and as he is ; who binds up wounds that are deeper and more terrible than any brigand's knife can inflict ; who brings him out of the place of danger to a place of security and peace, and provides for all his future needs. And all this without bargain or condition, and unconstrained by any motive save His own infinite compassion.

How one longs that honest-minded men like the author of "The Creed of Christendom" could be brought at least to *hear* these truths and to know that *this* is the gospel of Christianity! Their writings give proof that here in Christian England there are persons of enlightenment and culture whose most legitimate revolt against priestcraft and everything of mere religion has thrown them back into pagan darkness. But in the midst of this darkness light is shining. The agnostic's version of "Christ's grand and simple creed" would make Pharisees of some men—and heaven is absolutely closed to such—while it would relegate mankind in general to the position of hopeless and desperate outlawry. But Holy Scripture testifies that "Christ died for the *ungodly*," and that the man who believes in Him is justified.

And believing in Him has nothing in common with "accepting a string of metaphysical propositions." It means bowing to the Divine judgment upon sin, and accepting Christ as Saviour and Lord. Distrust was the turning-point in the creature's fall, for the overt act of sin was but the fruit of unbelief. How natural, then, that trust should be the turning-point in his recovery! There was a time in England when the wearing of a certain flower was the recognised avowal of loyalty or treason. And this was a mere outward act which might be insincere, whereas a man's beliefs are part and parcel of himself. The tragedy of Calvary has come to be regarded as a mere incident in history, natural in the circumstances, and fitted to emphasise and enhance the dignity of man. God points to it as the world's " crisis," an event of such stupendous moment that, in view of it, indifference is impossible. He who died there does not seek either our pity or our patronage : He claims our *faith*. It is a question of personal loyalty to Himself.

But this chapter is a digression. Let us turn to the teaching of the Epistle to the Romans.

10

MYSTERY NOW MANIFESTED

POSTSCRIPTS are proverbially important, and apostolic postscripts are no exception to the rule. But the final postscript to St. Paul's Epistle to the Romans has been treated with strange neglect by theologians. Witness the extraordinary carelessness with which it has been translated even by the Revisers of 1881! With his own hand it was, no doubt, that, after his secretary, Tertius, had laid down the pen, the apostle added the pregnant words which end the Epistle : "Now to Him that is able to stablish you according to my gospel even the preaching of Jesus Christ according to [the] revelation of a mystery which hath been kept in silence through times eternal, but now is manifested and by

prophetic scriptures according to the command-
ment of the Eternal God is made known unto all
the nations unto obedience of faith—to the only
wise God through Jesus Christ be the glory for
ever." [1]

" My Gospel." The words, three times repeated
by St. Paul,[2] are no mere conventional expression.
They are explained in several of his Epistles,[3] and
with peculiar definiteness in his letter to the Galatians. He there declares in explicit and emphatic
terms that the gospel which he preached among the
Gentiles was the subject of a special revelation
peculiar to himself. Not only was he not taught
it by those who were apostles before him, but he it
was who, by Divine command, communicated it to
"the twelve"; and this was not until his second visit

[1] Our English versions have distorted the passage, first by a punc-
tuation (I have followed Dean Alford's), which makes the mystery a
characteristic of the power to stablish us, whereas it characterises
the preaching by which we are stablished ; and secondly, by their
rendering of the words διά τε γραφῶν προφητικῶν (cf. Matt.
xxvi. 56, "*the* scriptures of *the* prophets"). It claims notice also
that both "revelation" and "mystery" are anarthrous ; but while the
English idiom seems to require the article before the former word,
its insertion before "mystery" is not only unnecessary, but mis-
leading.

[2] Rom. ii. 16, xvi. 25 ; 2 Tim. ii. 8.

[3] See, *e.g.*, Eph. iii.; Col. i. 25, 26.

to Jerusalem, seventeen years after his conversion.[1]
It is certain, therefore, that his testimony was essentially distinct in character and scope from anything
we shall find in the ministry of the other apostles,
as recorded in the Acts. And this, he declares,
they themselves acknowledged. "They saw," he
says, "that the gospel of the uncircumcision was
committed unto me, as the gospel of the circumcision was unto Peter."[2] The latter was a promise
according to the Scriptures of *the* prophets: the
former, a proclamation according to the revealing
of a mystery kept secret from eternity, but now
manifested in this Christian dispensation, and by
prophetic Scriptures made known to all nations.
What, then, were those writings? What the
mystery which was thus revealed?

The rendering of the passage in our English
versions is a compromise between translation and
exegesis; and that the exposition thus suggested
is erroneous is clear from the fact that it makes
the apostle's statement inconsistent to the verge of
absurdity. If it be by the writings of the Hebrew
prophets that the gospel is made known to all the

---

[1] Gal. i. 11–ii. 12.   [2] Ibid. ii. 7.

nations, it certainly was not a mystery kept secret through all the ages! The words "by prophetic writings" refer, of course, to the Scriptures of the *New* Testament; and as the gospel thus made known was entrusted, not even to the other apostles, but only to "the apostle of the Gentiles," it is, again of course, to the Epistles of Paul that we must turn to seek for it. Do these Epistles, then, contain any great characteristic truth or truths which cannot be found in the earlier Scriptures?

Our English word "mystery" means something which is either incomprehensible or unknown; but this is not the significance of the Greek *musterion.*[1] In its primary meaning in classical and Biblical Greek it is simply a secret; and a secret when once disclosed may be understood by any one. A patent lock is a "mystery." It is as easily opened as any other, provided we have the proper key, but without the key it cannot be opened at all. The mysteries of the New Testament are Divine truths which till then had been "kept in silence"; truths which had not been revealed in the earlier Scriptures, and which, until revealed, could not be known. Once

[1] See Appendix, Note V.

and once only, the word was used by the Lord Himself, as recorded in the three first Gospels, and it occurs four times in the Apocalypse. But with these exceptions it is found only in St. Paul's Epistles, where it occurs no fewer than twenty times.

In some of these passages the word is used in a secondary sense. In others, definite secrets are revealed. And notably we find the following :—

The mystery of Lawlessness, culminating in the revelation of the Lawless One.[1]

The mystery that at the coming of the Lord some of His people will pass to heaven, as Elijah did, "with death untasted and the grave unknown."[2]

The mystery that in the present dispensation believers are united to Christ in a special relationship as members of a body of which He Himself is the head.[3]

Here, then, we have specific "mysteries" respecting which the earlier Scriptures are silent; and it may be added that, though now revealed, they are

---

[1] 2 Thess. ii. 7, 8. Within the Church, of course. Lawlessness in the world is as old as sin.

[2] 1 Cor. xv. 51.   [3] Eph. iii. 4, 6, v. 30, 32 ; 1 Cor. xii. 12, 13, &c.

still unknown to the majority of Christians. But these are truths essentially for the *believer*, whereas the " mystery " of the apostle's postscript is emphatically a truth for ALL—a truth to be "made known to all the nations for the obedience of faith."

The apostle's statement, moreover, assumes that his words would be understood by those to whom they were addressed. Therefore, as he had never personally visited Rome, we may confidently turn to the Epistle itself to find within it the truth referred to.

First, then, it is a *mystery* truth—a truth which till then had been "kept in silence." Secondly, it is a truth of universal scope and application. And thirdly, it is a truth to be found in the Epistle to the Romans. With these clews to guide us there can be no difficulty in fixing upon the truth which is here in question ; for one, and only one, will satisfy these requirements.

In common with some other great truths of the Christian faith,Reconciliation has received but scant notice from theologians. Many a page might be filled with quotations from standard books which either misrepresent or deny it. But all attempts to oust it from our creeds rest, as Archbishop Trench declares, "on a foregone determination to get rid of the reality of God's anger against sin."[1] Sin not merely alienated man from God, it alienated God from man. A just and holy God could not but regard him as an enemy. But "while we were enemies we were reconciled to God by the death of His Son." And "through our Lord Jesus Christ" they who believe "have now received the reconciliation."[2] "All things are of God who reconciled us to Himself through Christ, and gave unto us the ministry of the reconciliation, to wit, that God was in Christ reconciling the world unto Himself, not reckoning unto them their trespasses, and having committed unto us the word of the reconciliation. We are ambassadors, therefore, on behalf of Christ," the apostle adds, "as though God were entreating by us, we beseech men on behalf of Christ, 'be ye reconciled to God'"[3]—an appeal to the sinner, not,

---

[1] "Synonyms," Part II. p. 123. [2] Rom. v. 10, 11.

[3] 2 Cor. v. 18–20. This passage is inseparably associated in my mind with an incident once narrated to me by the late Sir Robert Lush. When Serjeant Wilkins returned to the Law Courts after an illness which practically ended his career, Mr. Lush (as he then was)

as too commonly represented, to forgive his God, but to come within the unsought benefit which God in His infinite grace has accomplished. For (the apostle further adds) "Him who knew no sin He made to be sin on our behalf, that we might become the righteousness of God in Him." [1]

Words could not be simpler, and yet, as already noticed, the truth so plainly taught is in many quarters perverted or denied. Just as in our day there are doctrinaire philanthropists who talk of crime as though it were nothing but a natural eccentricity of weak natures, so there are theologians who delight in such representations of sin that if provision had not been made for it in the Divine economy the omission would be entirely to the discredit of

saw him sitting with his face in his hands, and he noticed that tears were falling from between his fingers. The Serjeant was not of his acquaintance, but when he saw him hurriedly leave the court, he followed him, and delicately referring to what he had seen, he asked if he was in any trouble in which he could be of service to him. The Serjeant gratefully acknowledged his kindness, but explained his seeming distress by the fact that the words above quoted, which he had been reading that morning, had come back to his mind as he sat in court, and he could not restrain his emotion. The incident will be appreciated by those who know the sort of man he was. Suffice it to say it had not been his habit to read the Bible. But how many such there are who turn to it in times of sickness or trouble !

[1] 2 Cor. v. 21.

the Deity. Others, again, so fritter away the great truths of Divine love to the world and the reconciliation of the world to God through Christ, that the sovereignty of God degenerates into mere favouritism, and the death of Christ is no more than a means by which the favoured few can attain to blessing.

This great truth of Reconciliation will be sought in vain in the Old Testament Scriptures. The revelation of it, indeed, was impossible so long as the Jew held the position which he forfeited by rejecting the Messiah. Reading the Gospel of John in the light of the Epistles we can discern it in the teaching of our Lord ; but without that light no one would dare to formulate it. To the Jew, indeed, the doctrine must have been astounding, and even among Christians it is received with hesitation and reserve. But the difficulties which beset the exposition of the fifth chapter of Romans relate only to the *argument*. The doctrine it teaches is unequivocally clear. " As through one trespass [the result was] unto all men to condemnation ; even so through one act of righteousness [the result was] unto all men to justification of life." If words have any meaning this declares that the death of Christ has efficacy as complete and universal as the sin of Adam. If that sin "brought death into the world, and all our woe," so the great *dikaiōma* brought justification of life to all men in so far as the Eden trespass brought condemnation to them.

But the work of Christ goes infinitely further than this. The Eden trespass ushered in the reign of sin. "Sin reigned unto death." "The wages of sin is death," and sin claimed the very throne of God as an agency for enforcing its just demands. But Calvary has dethroned sin, and grace now reigns supreme. And this, not at the expense of righteousness, but through righteousness. And as sin reigned unto death, so grace now reigns unto eternal life. Or, getting behind the magnificent imagery of the Epistle, we grasp the amazing truth that the Divine attitude toward men is one of universal beneficence. It is not that the Gentile has attained to the special position of privilege from which the Jew has fallen, for apart from "the household of faith" there is no favoured people now. "There is no distinction between Jew and Greek, for the same Lord is Lord of all, and is rich unto all that call upon Him; for *whosoever* shall call upon the name of the Lord shall be saved."[1]   Eternal life is thus brought within reach of every human being to whom this testimony comes.[2]   How, then, is it possible that so few receive the benefit?   The answer to this question claims a chapter to itself.

[1] Rom. **x. 12** (R.V.).

[2] Such a statement will be resented by that school of religious thought which boasts as its founder one of the greatest of the Church's teachers.   But let us appeal from the disciples to their master.   Here is Calvin's commentary upon the verse above quoted (Rom. **v. 18**).   "He makes this favour common to all because it is propounded to all, and not because it is in reality extended to all; for though Christ suffered for the sins of the whole world, and is offered through God's benignity indiscriminately to all, yet all do not receive Him."

And the following extract from his commentary on the third chapter of the Gospel of St. John is no less apposite.   Referring to the sixteenth verse he says : "Christ employed the universal term *whosoever* both to invite indiscriminately all to partake of life, and to cut off every excuse from unbelievers.   Such is the import of the term *world*.   Though there is nothing in the world that is worthy of God's favour, yet He shows Himself to be reconciled to the whole world when He invites all men without exception to the faith of Christ, which is nothing else than an entrance into life."

And if any one ask, How, then, is Judgment possible? the answer is that Judgment is based upon this very truth.   See **c. xii.** *post.*

11

SATAN'S INFLUENCE

THE devil of Christendom is a myth. Just as human fancy, working on a basis of fact and truth, has impersonated an object for its worship, so by a like process it has created a scapegoat to account for the crimes and vices of humanity. A mythical Jesus is the Buddha of Christendom; a mythical Satan is its bogey. In the one case as in the other a gulf separates the myth from the reality.

The Satan of Christian mythology is a monster of wickedness, the instigator to every crime of exceptional brutality or loathsome lust. The Satan of Scripture is the awful being who dared to offer his patronage to our Divine Lord. When a man is led into evil courses " he is drawn away by his own lust." [1]   The human heart, our Lord Himself declares, is the vile spring from which immoralities and crimes proceed. [2]   Using the word "immoral" in its narrow, popular sense, there is no basis for the belief that Satan ever provokes to an immoral act.   Indeed, if we leave out of account his incitements aimed against Christ personally, the solitary instance of Ananias and Sapphira alone affords a pretext for asserting that he ever tempted any one to do anything which human judgment would condemn. [3]

This statement may seem startling, but it is true, and its truth can be established.   Of the unseen world we know absolutely nothing beyond what Scripture reveals : to the Scriptures, therefore, we must turn.   And here the Old Testament is eloquent by reason of its silence.   If the popular belief were well founded, is it possible that from Genesis to Malachi not a word could be found in support of it?   In three passages only is Satan mentioned.   The first describes the fall of man, and there the entire aim of the tempter was to alienate

---

[1] James i. 14   [2] Mark vii. 21.

[3] See Appendix, Note VI.

the creature from God. In the *rôle* of philanthropist he appeared to our first parents, and sowed in their hearts the seeds of distrust.[1] The next passage describes his assaults on Job, and here again his only aim was to lead the patriarch to doubt the Divine goodness.[2] And the third narrates that mysterious incident in which he sought to hinder the high priest Joshua in the discharge of his sacred office.[3]

When we turn to the New Testament we must avoid the popular error of confounding Satan with the angels that " kept not their own principality, but left their own habitation."[4] These are in bonds, awaiting " the judgment of the great day." They have no part in the course of human affairs. Demons, again, are beings of a wholly different order. It is assumed that they are subordinate to

[1] Gen. ii.   [2] Job i. ; ii.

[3] Zech. iii. **1, 2.** In **1** Chron. xxi. i and Psa. cix. 6, the word rendered Satan in A.V. is merely *an adversary*. And I cannot avail myself of Isa. xiv. 12, &c., and Ezek. xxviii. 14, &c., much as they would help me, because there is no way of ascertaining certainly whether Satan is there intended. I have no doubt of it myself. The word *Devil* does not occur in the Old Testament. In the four places where " Devils " is used in A.V. the R.V. adopts other words.

[4] Jude 6 ; **2** Pet. ii. 4.

the devil, and as some of them are expressly called "*unclean* spirits," uncleanness is attributed to Satan. But the assumption is based in part upon Jewish beliefs, and, even if a true one, the inference is forced. A ruler may have vicious subjects and yet not himself be vicious! [1]

But are not sins described as "the works of the devil"? And what of the words, "He that doeth sin is of the devil"? Will the objector consider the definition of sin to which this refers—one of the only definitions in the Bible? "Sin is lawlessness."[2] The possession of an independent will is man's proud but perilous boast. His duty and safety and happiness alike demand that this will shall be subordinated to the will of God, and all revolt against the Divine will is sin. Lawlessness is its

[1] In Matt. xii. 24–27, our Lord neither adopted nor rejected the Jewish belief. How grotesque is the suggestion that at such a time He should have discoursed to them on demonology! Passing the subject by, He turned their taunt back upon themselves by the words, "If I by Beelzebub cast out demons, by whom do your sons cast them out?" Unless the phenomena described by spiritualists may be explained by delusions or fraud, they must be attributed to demons; and there seems strong reason to believe that some men are possessed by "unclean" demons.

[2] 1 John iii. 4 (R.V.).

essence; the element of immorality is entirely accidental.

And this explains the apostolic comment upon the precept "Be angry and sin not."[1]   Anger may in itself be right.   But if cherished it is apt to degenerate into vindictiveness; and thus what in its inception may betoken fellowship with God—for "God is angry every day"[2]—may lead to thoughts and even acts which are only evil.   Therefore the apostle adds, "Let not the sun go down upon your wrath, neither give occasion to the devil."   The Satan myth leads men to read this as though it were no more than a warning against homicidal violence.   But the closing passage of this same Epistle[3] gives proof that the apostle's theology of Satanic temptations relates to a far different sphere.   The normal conflict of the Christian life begins where the struggle with "flesh and blood" has ceased.   It is in the spiritual sphere, and not in the domain of morals, that the panoply of God is needed.   The Pharisee or the

[1] Eph. iv. 26.   The words are quoted *verbatim* from Psa. iv. 4 (LXX).

[2] Psa. vii. 11.   [3] Eph. vi. 10–20.

Buddhist can boast as high a standard of morality as the Christian. Their motives may be lower, but the outward results are the same. When some man of repute is betrayed into acts of shame, the devil would be held accountable for his fall in any ecclesiastical court. But not at the Old Bailey, where prejudice avails nothing, and proof must be full and clear. No one may assert that Satan might not stoop to such means to attain his ends, but we may aver that no " previous conviction " is recorded to his prejudice.

" But," the objector will indignantly demand, "did not our Lord Himself denounce him as a liar and a murderer ? " Yes truly, such were His words to the Pharisees who were plotting His death. But what is their significance ? Let us consider them with open minds, for the Satan myth has so obscured their meaning that the commentaries will not help us. To the Jews' vain boast of their descent from Abraham, the Lord replied that the patriarch's children would walk in their father's ways ; but as for them, they sought to kill Him because He had spoken to them God-given truth. They then fell back upon that figment of the apostate, the fatherhood of God, thus bringing on themselves the scathing words, " Ye are of your father the devil, and the desires of your father it is your will to do. He was a murderer from the beginning and has not stood in the truth because truth is not in him. When he speaketh THE lie he speaketh of his own, for he is a liar and the father of IT." [1] These, remember, are not words of vulgar invective. They are the words of Christ Himself to men of character and repute, honourable and earnest men who, under their responsibilities as the religious leaders of the people, deplored His teaching as pestilent and profane. Such language addressed by such lips to such men is awful in its solemnity ; but what does it mean?

The devil was " a murderer from the beginning." The beginning of what? Not of his own existence, surely, for he was created in perfection and beauty. Nor yet of the Eden paradise, for Satan had dragged down others in his ruin long before our earth became the home of man. His being a murderer connects itself immediately with

[1] John viii. 44. See Appendix, Note VII.

THE truth which he has refused and THE lie of which he is the father. As we listen to these solemn and mysterious words of our Divine Lord we are accorded a glimpse into a past eternity when the great mystery of God was first made known to " principalities and powers," the great intelligences of the heavenly world.[1] Greatest of them all was the being whom now we know as Satan, and the promulgation of the purpose of the ages disclosed to him the fact that a First-born was yet to be revealed who was " in all things to have the pre-eminence."

Science has poured contempt upon the old belief that man is the centre of the universe. And yet the old belief was right. But He who claims this transcendent dignity is not the man of Eden—" vain insect of an hour ! "—but the Man who is " the Lord from Heaven." And He

---

[1] This is probably the explanation of the " coincidences " between Christianity and some of the old religions of the world. I do not allude to Buddhism, for its seeming " coincidences " admit of a much more prosaic explanation (see, *e.g.*, Professor Kellogg's work referred to at p. 68 *ante*, note) but to the cult of Tammuz and ancient Babylon. Scripture warns us that in the future Satan will travesty the Divine mysteries ; is it strange if he has done so in the past ?

it is who is the object of the devil's hate. In
compassing the fall of Adam he may perchance
have imagined that *he* was the promised first-born.
But it was not till the Temptation of Christ Himself that Satan and his lie were at last revealed.
Not one person in a thousand of those who read
the record of it attempts to realise its significance.
How could the Satan of Christendom dare to
stand before the Lord of Glory! And how could
the suggestions of such a loathsome monster be
anything but hateful and repulsive? Suppose the
biographer of some noble-minded and holy woman
sought to emphasise the purity of her mind and
the steadfastness of her character by recording
that she was once closeted with a man well known
to her as a coarse and shameless libertine, and
yet passed through the ordeal unscathed! No less
preposterous does the narrative of the temptation
appear if we read it in the false light of the
Satan myth.[1]

The Satan of Scripture is a being who claimed
to meet our Lord on more than equal terms.
Having "led Him up" and given Him that

[1] See Appendix, Note VI.

mysterious vision of earthly sovereignty, "the devil said unto Him," we read, "To Thee will I give all this authority and the glory of them; for it hath been delivered unto me, and to whomsoever I will I give it. If thou therefore wilt worship before me it shall all be thine."

Is this no more than the raving of irresponsible madness or impious profanity? It is the bold assertion of a disputed right. Satan claims to be the First-born, the rightful heir of creation, the true Messiah, and as such he claims the worship of mankind. Men dream of a devil, horned and hoofed—a hideous and obscene monster — who haunts the squalid slums and gilded vice-dens of our cities, and tempts the depraved to acts of atrocity or shame. But, according to Holy Writ, he "fashions himself into an angel of light," and "his ministers fashion themselves as ministers of righteousness." [1] Do "ministers of righteousness" corrupt men's morals or incite them to commit outrages?

And this prepares the way for the further statement that it is the *religion* of the world

[1] 2 Cor. xi. 14.

that he controls, and not its vices and its crimes. "The god of this world" is his awful title—a title Divinely conceded to the Evil One, not because the Supreme has delegated His sovereignty, but because the world accords him its homage. It is in the sphere of religion, then, that the influence of the Tempter is to be sought — not in the records of our criminal courts, not in the pages of obscene novels, but in the teaching of false theologies.

The lie of which he is the father is the denial of the Christ of God, the Christ of Calvary, the only mediator between God and men, the propitiation for the world's sins—the "mercy-seat" [1] where an outcast sinner can meet a holy God and find pardon and peace. But "the god of this world hath blinded the minds of the unbelieving that the light of the gospel of the glory of Christ, who is the image of God, should not dawn upon them." [2] Hence it is that men turn to the Church,

---

[1] In 1 John ii. 2, and iv. 10 He is called the ἱλασμός. In Rom. iii. 25 He is called the ἱλαστήριον (mercy-seat). The word occurs but once again in the New Testament, i.e., Heb. ix. 5.

[2] 2 Cor. iv. 4 (R.V.).

to religion, to morality, to "the Sermon on the Mount"—making the Lord Himself minister to their self-righteousness and pride—in a word, to anything and everything rather than to the Cross of Christ.

What led to the discovery of the planet Neptune was the apparent disturbance from some unknown cause in the movements of other planets. And have we not reason to search for a "Neptune" in the spiritual sphere? Is it not clear that there is some sinister influence in operation here? How else can it be explained that in the full light of our advanced civilisation, even persons of the highest intelligence and culture are gulled by the tricks and superstitions which form the stock-in-trade of priestcraft?

But "the lie" has other phases. The mind of the Tempter is disclosed no less in some of our most popular books of piety. Eternal judgment and a hell for the impenitent, redemption by blood, and the need of salvation through the death of the great Sin-bearer—these and kindred doctrines are rejected as survivals of a dark and credulous age : it is for man to work out his own destiny, and to raise himself to the Divine ideal. And all this is prefaced and made plausible by boldly insinuating that plain words Divinely spoken are either misunderstood or spurious. A new gospel some men call this : it is the oldest gospel known. In every point it reminds us of the old, old words: " Hath God said ? " " Ye shall *not* surely die : " " Ye shall be as gods knowing good and evil." The " Jesus " of this theology bears a sinister resemblance to the great philanthropist of Eden ! In the name of that " other Jesus " [1] the Christ of God would be again rejected if He returned to earth to-day.

During His ministry on earth the Lord's acts and words to the fallen and depraved led to His being branded as the friend of the dishonest and the immoral. And why? This question is best answered by another : Did He not come to seek and to save *the lost?* How then could He drive them from His presence ? A strange Saviour such would be ! *Sin* He could not tolerate, but for *sinners* His love and pity were infinite. And His detractors mistook sympathy with sinners for sympathy with sin. But when men refused to own that they were lost,

[1] 2 Cor. xi. 4.

and separated themselves from Him by an impassable barrier of religion and morality, infinite love was powerless. Omnipotence itself was baffled! And He who had wept in silence in presence of human sorrow gave way to unrestrained outbursts of grief as He contemplated their doom.[1]

On yet another occasion He exclaimed, " How often would I have gathered thy children together as a hen gathers her brood under her wings, and *ye would not.*"[2] The hand stretched out to save them they thrust from them with obloquy. And what wonder! Men of blameless morality, of the deepest piety, of intense devotion to religion— men looked up to and respected by the people, who acknowledged them as leaders, were told that the degraded and depraved had better hopes of heaven than themselves. His teaching was a public scandal; His mission was an insult to them. And all truth and decency were outraged when He openly called them " children of hell," and told them they had the devil for their father!

---

[1] In John xi. 35 the word used betokens silent tears. The word in Luke xix. 41 means to lament with every outward expression of grief.

[2] Luke xiii. 34.

When a malignant tumour is eating at the vitals the tenderness of the physician is useless ; the surgeon's knife must reach the mischief, let the risk be what it may. And surely if He who was so gracious, so "meek and lowly in heart," spoke such scathing words as these, it was because no tenderer treatment could avail. It was because their own case was desperate, and their influence was disastrous. And such men must have successors and representatives on earth to-day. Who are they, then? and where? Let the thoughtful reader work out the answer for himself. But let him keep in view the factors of the problem. It was not the "publicans and harlots" who were branded thus as hell-begotten. Alas for human nature, no devil was needed to account for the sins of such ! But to the *religious* Jews it was that these awful words were spoken. And why? Because the Satan cult is to be sought for, not in pagan orgies, but in the acceptance of the Eden gospel, and the pursuit of religious systems, which honour man and dishonour Christ. [1]

---

[1] For a further discussion of the general question, see Appendix, Note VIII.

12

GRACE AND JUDGMENT

EVERYBODY knows the little girl who, having heard her father complain that his watch needed cleaning, stole away to clean it in a basin of soap-suds! The story is but a grotesquely exaggerated instance of what we all suffer from—ignorant zeal, unintelligent desire to please. No one but a brute would vent his anger on his baby, when, with eyes sparkling and cheeks flushed at the thought of having done a kind and useful service, she brings him his ruined watch. But if this were done by one who ought to have known better, no such restraint would be called for. To this every one will assent; but no one seems to take account of similar considerations in our relations with the Deity.

"The chief end of man is to glorify and enjoy himself for ever." Such is the present-day reading of the first great thesis in the catechism of the Westminster Divines.[1] And to attain this end man wants a religion and a god, just as a prince needs a private chaplain. But a chaplain should know his place, and not intrude where his presence would be embarrassing. And so with God. It is intolerable that He should claim to decide in what way alone we can please Him. In leading moral and religious lives we "render to God the things that are God's." And we must not forget what is due to ourselves. But "the chief end of man is to glorify GOD." This is what the Westminster Divines really wrote; but that was long ago, and the Westminster Divines were ignorant, and knew nothing of "the gospel of humanity"!

In a word, God claims our homage, and we offer Him our patronage. He claims the undivided devotion of our life, and we offer Him religion and

[1] "The Scotch Catechism" it is commonly called, as though Westminster were somewhere north of the Tweed! This catechism was compiled by pious and learned "Dons" of Cambridge University, and adopted by "an assembly of learned and godly divines" convened in Westminster Abbey.

morality. But God does not want our patronage;
neither does He want either our morality or our
religion. " Monstrous ! " the reader will exclaim,
preparing to throw down the volume. " Is it a
matter of indifference whether we are moral and
religious, or not?" By no means a matter of
indifference as regards *ourselves :* not even as to
our life on earth, to say nothing of the judgment
to come. But of supreme indifference to God.
The man who struts about, inflated by the conceit
begotten of humanity gospels, is like the Jew who
supposed he was doing the Most High a benefit
when he piled " the fat of fed beasts " [1] upon His
altar—the altar of the " God who made the world
and all things that are therein."

Strange though it may seem, God has a purpose
and a will ; and He is so unreasonable as to require
the recognition of that purpose, and compliance
with that will. But these are matters of revelation ; and, therefore, here once again the ways
divide. Human religion in every phase of it is of
interest to men, and books about it will be read,
noticed, and discussed. But Christianity is a

[1] Isa. i. 11.

Divine revelation, and, therefore, to use a popular vulgarism, it is "boycotted." But in the great truths of Christianity, now so little known, is to be found the only true philosophy, the only true solution of the deeper problems of life, which so perplex and grieve us.

God's judgments are righteous. And the principles which govern them are clearly stated: He "will render to every man according to his deeds: to them who, by patient continuance in well-doing, seek for glory and honour and immortality, eternal life." [1] Who will question the equity of this? The story is told of Bishop Wilberforce, that a Hampshire railway porter, a hedge theologian of local fame, tried to pose him with the question, "What is the way to heaven?" "The way to heaven?" said the bishop, as the train in which he was seated moved out of the station— "turn to the *right*, and keep straight on!" But what is the right? This is the vital question. And this every man claims to settle for himself. Whatever reason and conscience declare to be right *is* right—this is a maxim almost universally

[1] Rom. ii. 6, 7.

accepted. And in the absence of a revelation, it is, within certain limits, practically true. But when the Supreme makes known His will, compliance with that will becomes the test of well-doing.

In the Mosaic economy, religion and morality had prominence. And in the cult of Christendom, which, in one aspect of it, is but a corrupted form of Judaism, disguised by Christian phraseology, religion and morality are everything. But the era of religion and morality is past. These were like guides which were followed in the darkness till the goal was reached to which they led. The Mosaic economy was a state of tutelage which ended with the coming of Christ. To set up morality and religion now is to bring ourselves within the denunciation of the words which follow in the passage quoted : " But unto them that are contentious, and do not obey the truth, but obey unrighteousness, indignation and wrath." Hence the Lord's reply to the question, " What shall we do that we might work the works of God ? " " This," He replied, " is the work of God, that ye believe on Him whom He hath sent." [1] " Then a

[1] John vi. 28, 29.

man may be as immoral as he likes, provided only
he 'believes,' as you call it." Such is the rejoinder
of the contentious. Such was the criticism of those
who heard His words. Reason told them it was
wrong ; and clinging to their morality and religion,
instead of believing in "the Sent One," they
crucified Him.

To set up an altar "to an unknown God" is the
highest possible attainment of natural religion.
But as St. Paul said at Athens,[1] even the light of
nature should teach men that God does not want
our service or our patronage "as though He needed
anything." He wished men to seek Him, even
though they had need to grope for Him blindly
and in darkness—"to feel after Him and find
Him." And He could give them blessing in
spite of ignorance, for "He is a rewarder of diligent seekers." If they but "turned to the right
and kept straight on," He could, as St. Paul
declared, overlook the ignorance. "But now,"
he goes on to say, "He commandeth all men
everywhere to repent." And the change depends on this, that God has revealed Himself

[1] Acts xvii. 22–31.

in Christ, and therefore ignorance of His will is sin that shuts men up to judgment. A new era has dawned upon the world. "The Word was made flesh and dwelt among us." The darkness is past, the true light is shining. To turn now to conscience or to law—to religion and morality—is to act like men who, with the sun in the zenith, keep shutters barred and curtains drawn. The principle on which God deals with men is the same, but the measure of man's responsibility is entirely changed. Such was the great truth so plainly stated by our Divine Lord in His words to Nicodemus. This, He declared, was the condemnation, not that men's deeds were evil—though for these there shall be wrath in the day of wrath—but that, because their deeds were evil, they had brought upon themselves a still direr doom : light had come into the world, but they turned from it and *loved* the darkness.

Men cannot and will not believe that the great controversy between them and God is altogether about Christ. To most men, indeed, the very statement seems to savour of mysticism. The death of Christ is one of the commonplaces of the philosophy, as well as of the theology, of Christendom. Men boast of it as the highest tribute to human worth. But God's estimate of it is vastly different. "The Son of God has died by the hands of men! This astounding fact is the moral centre of all things. A bygone eternity knew no other future; an eternity to come shall know no other past. That death was the world's crisis. For long ages, despite conscience outraged, the light of nature quenched, law broken, promises despised, and prophets cast out and slain, the world had been on terms with God. But now a tremendous change ensued. Once for all the world had taken sides. In the midst stood that cross in its lonely majesty: God on one side with averted face; on the other Satan, exulting in his triumph. And the world took sides with Satan." [1]

And in presence of that cross God calls upon every one to whom the record comes to declare himself on the one side or the other. But men struggle to evade the issue. Many, of course, ignore it altogether in a selfish or a vicious life; but not a few attempt a compromise by

[1] "The Gospel and its Ministry," p. 12.

turning to religion. But so far as this supreme question is concerned the result is the same for all. What the end will be of those who never heard of Christ we know not. But there is neither reserve nor mystery in Scripture as to what the portion will be of those who "obey the gospel" and of those who reject it. Upon that choice depends the eternal destiny of each. Hence the virulence with which the Bible is attacked; for if Christ be beyond our reach our responsibility is at an end. Some there are indeed who affect personal devotion to Himself though they disparage or despise the Scriptures. But every thoughtful person recognises that it is only through the record that we can reach the person, that it is only through the written Word that we can reach the Living Word. Hence His declaration: "He that rejecteth Me, and receiveth not My words, hath one that judgeth him: the word that I have spoken, the same shall judge him in the last day." [1]

The consequences, then, of accepting or rejecting Christ are eternal. No other question is open.

[1] John xii. 48.

Morality! In morals, as in physics, the greater includes the less, and the gospel teaches a higher morality than conscience and law combined. But in this Christian dispensation God is not imputing their sins to men. Were it otherwise the silence of Heaven would give place to the thunders of His judgments. Every question of judgment was either settled for ever at the Cross, or has been postponed to the day that is still to come: God "knows how" "to reserve the unjust to the day of judgment to be punished,"[1] and the day of judgment is not yet.

A red-letter day it must have seemed to the village community of Nazareth when the great Rabbi who had grown to manhood in their midst reappeared in their synagogue, and stood up to read the Sabbath lesson from the Prophets.[2] Opening the roll delivered to Him, He found the passage beginning, "The Spirit of the Lord is upon me, because He anointed me to preach good tidings to the poor; He hath sent me to proclaim release to the captives, and recovering of sight to the blind, to set at liberty them that

[1] 2 Pet. ii. 9.   [2] Luke iv. 16-22.

are bruised, to proclaim the acceptable year of the Lord——": and abruptly closing the book, He handed it back to the attendant and sat down. Having stood forward to read the lesson for the day, He stopped in the middle of the opening sentence. What wonder that all eyes were fastened on Him! "This day," He broke the silence by declaring, "is this Scripture fulfilled in your ears."

"And the day of vengeance of our God" were the words that followed without a break on the open page before Him; but He left those words unread. "The acceptable year of the Lord" He then and there proclaimed, and it still runs its course, but the great day of judgment is even now still future.

Not that the moral government of the world is in abeyance. Even here and now men reap what they sow. Righteousness prospers and iniquity brings its own penalty. Not always indeed, nor openly; but generally, and with sufficient definiteness to make it clear that this is the rule—the ordinary course of things. And further, in the Divine economy provision is made for human government; and the sword is entrusted to men that rulers may be a terror to the evil-doer and a protection to the good. Were it otherwise society would be impossible. But while men are thus empowered to punish offences against human laws, the judgment of *sin* is altogether with God.

And here we recall another declaration of our Divine Lord. "The Father judgeth no man, but hath committed all judgment unto the Son." "We believe that Thou shalt come to be our judge" is upon the lips of thousands who in their hearts imagine that He will mediate in the judgment between them and an offended God. But it is to the crucified One Himself that in virtue of the Cross the Divine prerogative of judgment has been assigned. And He, the sinner's only Judge, is now the sinner's Saviour. Purification for sins accomplished, He has "sat down on the right hand of the Majesty on high."[1] The official attitude of Christ, if such a phrase may be allowed, is one of rest. The work of redemption is complete. The great amnesty has

[1] Heb. i. 3.

been proclaimed. Heaven is thrown open to the lost of earth. Eternal life is brought within the reach of the weakest and the worst of men. God is not imputing trespasses, but preaching peace. And the only Being in the universe who has power to punish sin is now seated on the throne of God as Saviour, and His presence there has changed that throne into a throne of grace. Grace reigns through righteousness unto eternal life; for "the free gift of God is eternal life in Christ Jesus our Lord." [1]

" How monstrous all this is! The idea of supposing that people who have consistently lived religious lives are to be shut out of heaven, while the worthless and depraved can obtain forgiveness and acceptance simply by believing in Christ!" Such will be the criticism these statements will generally evoke. Monstrous it may seem; but before men hold it up to censure or ridicule let them pause and reflect what it is that they are thus rejecting. "To Him bear all the prophets witness that through His name every one that believeth on Him shall

[1] See Appendix, Note IX.

receive remission of sins." [1] Nor is it a dogma of " Pauline doctrine," but the teaching of one of the simplest parables of Christ, that waifs and tramps from the highways and the slums sit down in the Kingdom of God, while the once invited guests—the moral and religious—are excluded.[2] And the parable is explained by the doctrine that His Divine mission was " not to call the righteous, but sinners to repentance."

[1] Acts x. 43 (R.V.).   [2] Luke xiv. 15–24.

13

THE REIGN OF GRACE

A SILENT Heaven! Yes, but it is not the silence of callous indifference or helpless weakness; it is the silence of a great sabbatic rest, the silence of a peace which is absolute and profound—a silence which is the public pledge and proof that the way is open for the guiltiest of mankind to draw near to God. When faith murmurs, and unbelief revolts, and men challenge the Supreme to break that silence and declare Himself, how little do they realise what the challenge means! It means the withdrawal of the amnesty; it means the end of the reign of grace; it means the closing of the day of mercy and the dawning of the day of wrath.

Among the statements which distressed the orthodox in the late Professor Tyndall's famous Birmingham address on "Science and Man," was his reference to the Herald Angels' song. "Look to the East at the present moment" (he exclaimed) "as a comment on the promise of peace on earth and goodwill towards men. The promise is a dream ruined by the experience of eighteen centuries, and in that ruin is involved the claim of the 'heavenly host' to prophetic vision." But the angels' song was not a promise; still less was it a prophecy. That anthem of praise was a Divine proclamation. The time was not yet when God could enforce peace between man and man; but grace "came by Jesus Christ," and with that advent peace and goodwill became the attitude of God to men. And this "on earth," even in the midst of their sorrows and their sins. "He came and preached good tidings of peace."[1] And "he that has ears to hear" can catch the echo of that voice as it still vibrates in our air. If God is silent now it is because Heaven has come down to earth, the climax of Divine revelation has been reached, there is no reserve of mercy yet to be unfolded. He has spoken His last word of love and grace, and when next He

[1] Eph. ii. 17 (R.V. *marg.*).

breaks the silence it will be to let loose the judgments which shall yet engulf a world that has rejected Christ. For "our God shall come and shall *not* keep silence." [1]

A silent Heaven is a part of the mystery of God; but Holy Writ declares that a day is fixed in the Divine chronology when "the mystery of God shall be finished." [2] And when that day breaks, the heavenly host shall again be heard, proclaiming that "The sovereignty of the world [3] is become our Lord's and His Christ's, and He shall reign for ever and ever." And at this signal the wonderful beings that sit on thrones around the throne of God shall raise the anthem, "We give Thee thanks, O Lord God Almighty, which art, and wast, and art to come, because Thou hast taken to Thee Thy great power, and hast reigned. And the nations were angry and Thy wrath is come, and the time of the dead that they should be judged, and that Thou shouldest give reward to Thy servants the prophets and to the saints and them that fear Thy name,

[1] Psa. l. 3.   [2] Rev. x. 7.

[3] ἡ βασιλέια τοῦ κόσμου (Rev. xi. 15).

small and great, and shouldest destroy them that destroy the earth."[1] Then at last He will assume the power that even now is His by right, and openly reward the good and put down the evil. In a word, He will do then what men think He ought to do now and always. And if He delays to do this, it is not that He is "slack concerning His promise." God's own "apology" for His inaction is that He is "longsuffering to us-ward, not willing that any should perish, but that all should come to repentance."[2]

Through all the ages until Christ came the course of human history was an unanswered indictment by which every attribute of God was seemingly discredited. The Divine power and wisdom and righteousness and love were all brought into question. But the advent of Christ was God's full and final revelation of Himself to man. There are mysteries, no doubt, which still remain unsolved, but they are mysteries which lie beyond the horizon of our world. First among these is the origin

[1] Rev. xi. 15-18.   [2] 2 Pet. iii. 9.

of evil. Not the Eden fall, but the fall of that wonderful Being to whose "devices" the Eden fall was due. Why did God permit the first and noblest of His creatures to turn devil? But of all the questions which immediately concern us, there is not one which the Cross of Christ has left unanswered. Men point to the sad incidents of human life on earth, and they ask "Where is the love of God?" God points to that Cross as the unreserved manifestation of love so inconceivably infinite as to answer every challenge and silence all doubt for ever.[1] And that Cross is not merely the public proof of what God has accomplished ; it is the earnest of all that He has promised. The crowning mystery of God is Christ, for in Him "are all the treasures of wisdom and knowledge hidden."[2] And those hidden

[1] Anything which is manifest is of course raised out of the sphere of doubt or question ; and God declares that in the Cross of Christ His grace and kindness and love have been *manifested* (Tit. ii. 11, iii. 4 ; 1 John iv. 9). But, ignoring the stupendous fact that, for our sakes, He "spared not His own Son," men seek to put Him upon proof of His love ; and the test is whether He complies with some specific appeal urged in the petulance of present need or sorrow.

[2] Col. ii. 2, 3 (R.V.).

treasures are yet to be unfolded. It is the Divine purpose to "gather together in one all things in Christ."[1] Sin has broken the harmony of creation, but that harmony shall yet be restored by the supremacy of our now despised and rejected Lord. In the very name of His humiliation every knee in heaven and on earth and in the underworld shall bow before Him, and every tongue shall confess that He is Lord.[2]

And to believe in Christ is to own His Lordship *now*. Hence the promise, "If thou shalt confess with thy mouth Jesus as Lord, and shalt believe in thy heart that God raised Him from the dead, thou shalt be saved."[3] The sinner who thus believes in Christ anticipates now and here the realisation of the supreme purpose of God, and he is absolutely and for ever saved.

[1] Eph. i. 10.   [2] Phil. ii. 10.

[3] Rom. x. 9 (R.V.). The true Buddhist will declare himself by the way in which he names his master, never omitting some title expressive of his reverence for him. And the true Christian will declare himself in the same way. If a man habitually writes or speaks about "Jesus," we may be sure, whatever his creed may be, that he is a Socinian at heart. "That Jesus Christ is LORD" is the special testimony of Christianity, and the Christian will not forget it even in his words.

It was in the power of these truths that the martyrs lived and died. Here was the secret of their triumph—not "the general sense of Scripture corrected in the light of reason and conscience"; not the insolent pretensions of priestcraft, degrading to every one who tolerates them. With hearts awed by the fear of God, garrisoned by the peace of God, and exulting in the love of God, shed abroad there by the Divine Spirit, they stood for the truth against priests and princes combined, and daring to be called heretics they were faithful to their Lord in life and in death.

Heaven was as silent then as it is now. No sights were seen, no voice was heard, to make their persecutors pause. No signs were witnessed to give proof that God was with them as they lay upon the rack or gave up their life-breath at the stake. But with their spiritual vision focussed upon Christ, the unseen realities of heaven filled their hearts, as they passed from a world that was not worthy of them to the home that God has prepared for them that love Him. But with us, the degenerate sons of a degenerate age, faith falters beneath the strain of the petty trials of our life. And while He is saying " I will never leave thee nor forsake thee," our murmurs drown His voice ; and though professing to be " followers of them who through faith and patience inherit the promises," our petulance and unbelief put from us the infinite compassions of God.   " *They* endured as seeing Him who is invisible " : *we* can see nothing but our troubles and our sorrows, which loom the greater because viewed through tears of selfish grief, that blind our eyes to the glories of eternity.

The dispensation of law and covenant and promise—the distinctive privileges of the favoured people—was marked by the public display of Divine power upon earth. But the reign of grace has its correlative in the life of faith. Ours is the higher privilege, the greater blessedness of those "who have not seen and yet have believed."[1] And walking by faith is the antithesis of walking by sight. If "signs and wonders" were vouchsafed to us, as in Pentecostal days, faith would sink to a lower level, and the whole standard and character of the discipline of Christian life would be changed.[2]

[1] John xx. 29.   [2] See Appendix, Note X.

The sufferings of Paul denote a higher faith than "the mighty deeds" of his earlier ministry. Not until miracles had ceased, and he had entered on the path of faith as we now tread it, was it revealed to him that his life was to be "a pattern to them that should afterwards believe." [1]

And what a life it was! Here is the amazing record: "Of the Jews five times received I forty stripes save one. Thrice was I beaten with rods, once was I stoned, thrice I suffered shipwreck, a night and a day have I been in the deep; in journeyings often, in perils of waters, in perils of robbers, in perils by my own countrymen, in perils by the heathen, in perils in the city, in perils in the wilderness, in perils in the sea, in perils among false brethren; in weariness and painfulness, in watchings often, in hunger and thirst, in fastings often, in cold and nakedness." [2] And all this not only without a murmur, but with a heart exulting in God. Instead of grumbling at his infirmities he made a boast of them. Instead of repining at his persecutions

[1] 1 Tim. i. 16.   [2] 2 Cor. xi. 24–27.

he learned to take pleasure in them.[1] Not vainly nor morbidly, but "for Christ's sake," his Master and Lord, for whom, he declared, "he had suffered the loss of all things." Reviewing all his privations and sufferings he describes them as "light affliction which is for the moment, working for us more and more exceedingly an eternal weight of glory," and he adds, "while we look, not at the things which are seen, but at the things which are not seen; for the things which are seen are temporal, but the things which are not seen are eternal."[2]

How different this from the experience described in the opening chapter![3] There it is a case of those who, seeing nothing beyond the events and circumstances of their life, turn away

[1] Here is an ascending scale of experience:

"Hath God forgotten to be gracious? Hath He in anger shut up His tender mercies?" (Psa. lxxvii. 9).

"I was dumb, I opened not my mouth, because Thou didst it" (Psa. xxxix. 9).

"I have learned in whatsoever state I am therewith to be content" (Phil. iv. 11).

"Most gladly therefore will I rather glory in my infirmities . . . I take pleasure in infirmities, in reproaches, in necessities, in persecutions, in distresses for Christ's sake" (2 Cor. xii. 9, 10).

[2] 2 Cor. iv. 17, 18. [3] Page 10 *ante*.

from God with hardened and embittered hearts. But the sons of faith look away from the fierce waves and threatening storm-clouds, for well they know that–

> " Above the voice of many waters,
> The mighty breakers of the sea,
> The Lord on high is mighty." [1]

And thus, filled with glad thoughts of the home beyond and of the glory to which He is calling them, they can rejoice in Him, even though in heaviness in manifold trials, for the proof of their faith is precious.[2]

Men understand and appreciate the asceticisms of religion—"will-worship, and humility, and severity to the body"—penances and ordinances which are "after the precepts and doctrines of men." [3] But these have nothing in common with the life of faith. They are paths by which men delude themselves in vain efforts to reach the Cross. But it is at the Cross itself that the life of faith begins. And the spiritual

---

[1] Psa. xciii. 4 (R.V. *revised*. The word *voice* is in the plural, but it is obviously the Hebrew *poetical* plural: not several voices, but " the *great* voice ").

[2] 1 Pet. i. 6, 7.   [3] Col. ii. 23 (R.V).

miracles of that life are more wonderful than any which merely controlled or suspended the operation of natural laws. Greatest of them all is the miracle of the new birth by the Spirit of God, with its outward side of conversion from a life of selfishness or sin to a life of consecrated service. And those who have experienced it can say in the words of Holy Writ, "We know that the Son of God is come, and hath given us an understanding, that we may know Him that is true." [1] And carrying the truth to others, they find it produces the same results which they themselves have proved. And this not merely in isolated cases or in favouring circumstances. Recent years, during which so many who have publicly pledged their belief that the Bible is true, [2] and who are subsidised to teach that it is Divine, have been labouring to

[1] 1 John v. 20.

[2] Every candidate for ordination must publicly declare, in reply to the Bishop, that he " unfeignedly believes all the canonical Scriptures of the Old and New Testaments." Whether such a pledge ought to be required I will not discuss. The fact remains. And this being so, when *clergymen* set themselves to discredit the Bible, the primary question suggested concerns their own honesty. Has the Church a lower standard of morality than the Clubs?

prove that it is unreliable and human—these have been precisely the years in which Christian men have carried it to some of the most degraded races of the heathen world, with results that surpass all previous records, giving overwhelming proof of its Divine character and mission.

To men like these there is a sense in which Heaven is *not* silent. The science of to-day has taught us that there are rays of light, till now unknown, which can penetrate the densest substances. But these rays can only be evolved when the atmosphere of earth has been excluded. And such wonders have their counterpart in the spiritual sphere. Those who can thus escape from the influence of earth, and rise above the seen and temporal, have eyes to see and ears to hear the sights and sounds of another world; and with united voice they testify that God is with His people and that His Word is true.

And behind these men are tens of thousands of Christians at home, including not a few of the greatest theologians, and thinkers, and scholars of the age, who share their beliefs and rejoice in their triumphs. Not that the question, What is truth? can be settled by a *plebiscite!* For truth has always been in a minority. But there is no element of cohesion in error. Among the children of error there is no bond of unity save such as depends on common hostility to truth. One generation kills the prophets; another builds their sepulchres. Those who shed the martyrs' blood are repudiated and condemned by their successors and representatives to-day. But the children of truth in every age are one. Great is the "cloud of witnesses" encompassing us round—the righteous dead of all the ages past. And when our race shall have been run, we too in time shall pass from the arena to join the mighty throng, until at last, their ranks complete, the ever-swelling host shall stand, a countless multitude, before the throne of God.

What a success this book might have been had it but fulfilled the promise of its earlier pages! If only it had gone on to enforce the revolt against faith suggested in the opening chapter, then indeed it would have been "reviewed" in the newspapers and "called for" at the libraries. But while sceptical attacks upon the Bible rank with general literature,[1] any defence of it which appeals to its deeper teaching is deemed unsuited for notice in the secular press. And so it comes about that everything which unbelief has to urge is brought prominently before the public, but the vast majority of people never hear of a book which is distinctly Christian.

Religion and Scepticism are rival competitors for popular favour. And yet there are many who, though conscious of longings too deep to be satisfied by mere religion, make choice of religion because they know of no other refuge from unbelief. And there are others again who, "with too much knowledge for the sceptic's side," drift into scepticism in their recoil from priestcraft.[2] To some such, perchance, these pages may suggest a better way. For Christianity delivers us not

---

[1] Appendix, Note XI.

[2] The lives of the Newmans afford an apt illustration. Both made shipwreck of their faith—the one in religion, the other in infidelity. The "Apologia" and the "Phases of Faith" are among the saddest of books.

only from scepticism on the one hand, but from superstition on the other.

And to not a few this volume may be welcome as affording a clew to pressing difficulties which perplex and distress the thoughtful. Infidelity trades upon the silence of Heaven, the inaction of the Supreme. If there be a God, almighty and all-good, why does He not use His power and give proof of His goodness in the way men choose to expect of Him? The answer usually offered by the Christian apologist fails either to silence the opponent or to satisfy the believer. And rightly so, for it is lacking not only in cogency but in sympathy. The God of the Bible is infinite both in power and in compassion; and in other ages His people had public proof of this. Why, then, is He so silent?

The question is not why He does not *always* declare Himself, but why He *never* does so. If, as already urged, whole generations even passed away without experiencing any direct manifestation of Divine power on earth, then, in presence of some crushing sorrow, some hideous wrong, His people might well exclaim with Gideon long ago, "If the Lord be with us, why then is all this befallen us? and where be all His miracles which our fathers told us of?"[1] But what concerns us is the fact that throughout the entire course of this Christian dispensation since Pentecostal times, "the finger of God"[2] has never been openly at work upon earth, never once has a public miracle been witnessed—"a single public event to compel belief that there is a God at all!" Are we left to grope in darkness for the answer? Does revelation throw no light upon it? To suggest the solution of this mystery these pages have been written. It now remains but to recapitulate the argument they offer.

An appeal to "the Christian miracles," it has been urged, so far from solving the mystery, serves only to intensify it. The purpose of the miracles, moreover, was to accredit the Messiah to Israel, and not, as generally supposed, to accredit Christianity to the heathen. And therefore, as Scripture plainly indicates, they continued so long as the testimony was addressed to the Jew, but ceased when, the Jew being set aside, the gospel went out to the Gentile world.

[1] Judg. vi. 13.   [2] Luke xi. 20.

But the crisis which deprived the favoured nation of its vantage-ground of privilege was made the occasion of a new revelation to mankind. Israel's fall was "the reconciliation of the world."[1] God assumed a new attitude toward men. Mercy there had always been for Gentiles, for the diligent seeker after God never sought Him in vain.[2] But Christianity goes infinitely beyond this. It is the realisation of the change foreshadowed by the prophetic words, "I was found of them that *sought Me not;* I was made manifest unto them that asked not after Me."[3] It is not that God will give heed to the cry of the true penitent who entreats for mercy, for this He ever did, but that He Himself is entreating even the impenitent to turn to Him; He is beseeching men to be reconciled.[4] It is not that there is mercy for *some* men, but that God has now made a public declaration of His grace, "salvation-bringing to ALL men."[5]

---

[1] Rom. xi. 15.

[2] Acts xvii. 27; Heb. xi. 6; Rom. ii. 7. And see specially Acts x. 34, 35.

[3] Rom. x. 20.   [4] 2 Cor. v. 20.

[5] σωτήριος πᾶσιν ἀνθρώποις (Titus ii. 11).

Grace is on the throne, reigning through righteousness unto eternal life.[1]

But it is plain matter of fact that before this, the great characteristic truth of Christianity, was revealed there was immediate Divine intervention upon earth : in a word, there were miracles ; whereas, after this truth was revealed, they ceased. The era of the reign of grace is precisely the era of the silence of God. To grace, therefore, we look to explain the silence. Christianity is the supreme and final revelation of the Divine " kindness and love-toward-man." [2] Therefore when God again declares Himself it can only be in wrath, and wrath must await " the day of wrath." [3]

Not that human government has lost its Divine sanction, for " the powers that be are ordained of God." [4] Nor yet that the moral government of the world is in abeyance : the laws of nature are relentlessly enforced.[5] But in this higher sphere there is neither court nor constable empowered to deal with the sins of men ; for He to whom alone

---

[1] Rom. v. 21.   [2] φιλανθρωπία (Titus iii. 4).

[3] Rom. ii. 5.   [4] Rom. xiii. 1.

[5] As an infidel writer has somewhere said, " Nature knows nothing of any such foolery as ' forgiveness of sins.' "

belongs the high prerogative of judgment is now enthroned as SAVIOUR. God is no longer "imputing their trespasses" to men.[1] From the throne of the Divine Majesty there has gone forth the proclamation of pardon and peace, and this without condition or reserve. And now a silent Heaven gives continuing proof that this great amnesty is still in force, and that the guiltiest of men may turn to God and find forgiveness of sins and eternal life. God is silent because He has spoken His last word of mercy and love, and judgment must await the "day of judgment"— there can be no place for it in this "day of grace."[2]

---

[1] 2 Cor. v. 19. See pp. 111–116 *ante*, and App. Note VIII.

[2] In proportion to our appreciation of the Christian revelation will be our appreciation of the argument that God cannot now intervene, or declare Himself, directly and openly. But this leaves unanswered the difficulty that He so often fails to intervene *indirectly* on behalf of His own people. This is dealt with in pp. 152–158 *ante*. The life of faith has always been a life of trial, and it is so specially in this dispensation of a silent Heaven. But it is our joy to know that our Divine Lord "was in all points tempted like as we are, apart from sin" (Heb. iv. 15). The statement seems to involve a contradiction, for how could He be tempted as we are tempted if, as the added words ($\chi\omega\rho\grave{\iota}\varsigma$ $\dot{\alpha}\mu\alpha\rho\tau\acute{\iota}\alpha\varsigma$) imply, "throughout these temptations, in their origin, in their process, in their result, sin had nothing in Him; He was free and separate from it"? (Alford). The explanation will be found in what has here been unfolded (Chap. XI. *ante*) respecting Satanic temptations as

To many all this will seem the merest mysticism
Others, again, will see no meaning in it whatsoever.
For to them the ministry and death of Christ are
but a splendid episode which has raised humanity
to a higher level than it ever before attained. For
such, indeed, the problem of this book has no
significance.[1]   Having but a timid belief in the

primarily designed to destroy our confidence in God. The thirty
years before our Lord entered on His public ministry, spent in
enforced inaction in the midst of abounding sorrow and evil and
wrong, must have been to Him a living martyrdom, the Tempter
ever taunting Him with the seeming apathy of God. And when
we read that "He *suffered*, being tempted" (Heb. ii. 18), we can
realise how truly He was human, and how deep and real was His
humiliation.

[1] Such have been precisely the criticisms this volume has evoked.
One of the chief organs of cultured thought in England describes
it as "a book full of religious mysticism." And one of the leading
press organs of the "Sadducees," while speaking in flattering terms
of the way in which the problem of the book is stated, can see
nothing in the proposed solution of it. So it ever was. To the
Jew the gospel of Christ was an offence because it set aside religion ;
to the cultured Greek it was foolishness because it ignored what he
was pleased to call wisdom. The "philosopher" was thinking of
evolution and the upward progress of humanity, but the gospel
spoke to him of grace that would pardon his sins and of judgment
to come. If the leaders of the school of thought and teaching here
alluded to could only be brought to apprehend the truth this volume
contains, their whole position and testimony would be changed.
But their literature will be searched for it in vain. Such a statement is easily made, but if untrue it can as easily be answered ; let
the book be cited which refutes it.

supernatural, the absence of miracles excites in them neither wonder nor distress. But there are not a few, happily, who have learned to think of Calvary, not as an upward step in the inevitable progress of the race toward the goal of its high destiny, but as a tremendous crisis which has brought man's probation to an end, leaving him absolutely dependent upon Divine grace, or, if he rejects the proffered mercy, shutting him up to judgment. And such will form a worthier estimate of the clew here offered to the mystery of a silent Heaven.

APPENDICES

Note 1 (page 18)

IN these pages I am dealing only with miracles in the theological sense ; that is, with Divine miracles. The phenomena of Spiritualism I have never personally investigated ; but if genuine they are clearly miraculous, and to reject, on *a priori* grounds, the mass of evidence adduced in proof of them in books like Professor A. R. Wallace's "Miracles and Modern Spiritualism," seems to me to savour of the stupidity of unbelief. Assuming their genuineness, no Christian need hesitate to account for them by demoniacal agency. To attribute them to departed spirits is as unphilosophical as it is unscriptural. It would seem that in this Christian dispensation, when the third Person of the Trinity dwells on earth, demons are subject to restraints which were not imposed in a preceding age, but there is no reason to refuse belief in their presence or their power.

Religious miracles also claim a passing notice here. I do not allude to the tricks of priests, but to cases of extraordinary cures from serious illness ; and some at least of these appear to be supported by evidence sufficient to establish their truth. The phenomena of hysteria and mimetic disease will probably account for the majority of cases of the kind. Others again may be explained as instances of the power of the mind and will over the body. The diseases which are necessarily fatal are comparatively few. But when a patient gives up hope his chances of recovery are greatly reduced. On the other hand, the progress of disease may be controlled, and even checked, by some mastering influence or emotion which turns the patient's thoughts back to life, and makes him believe he is convalescent. But while the vast majority of seemingly miraculous cures may thus be explained on natural principles, there may perhaps be some which are genuine miracles. There are no limits to the possibilities of faith, and God may thus declare Himself at times.

There is nothing in this admission to clash with the concluding statement of my second chapter, that in our dispensation, unlike those which preceded it, there are no *public* events to compel belief in God. I am there dealing, not with the mere fact of miracles, but with their evidential value ; and if there have been miracles

in Christendom, that element is wanting in them.
I may add that among Christians it is pestilently
evil to make the exceptional experience of some
the rule of faith for all.   The Word of God is our
guide, and not the experience of fellow-Christians ;
and when this is ignored the practical consequences
are disastrous.   The annals of " faith-healing," as
it is called, are rich in cases of mimetic or hys-
terical disease, but about the spiritual wreckage
due to failures innumerable they are silent.

Note 2 (page 45)

According to the dictionary the primary meaning
of *religion* is " piety."   But this, of course, is entirely
personal and subjective.   In these pages I use the
word only in its original sense, in which alone it
occurs in our English Bible.   " How little ' religion '
once meant godliness, how predominantly it was
used for the *outward* service of God, is plain from
many passages in our Homilies, and from other
contemporary literature."   But though Archbishop
Trench, from whose " English Past and Present "
this sentence is quoted, suggests that such a use of
the word is now obsolete, I venture to maintain that
it is in this, its original, but now secondary, meaning that it is commonly used at the present day.

And I may appeal to the fact that the Revisers
have retained it even in Gal. i. 13, 14, where " the
Jews' religion " is twice given as the equivalent

of "Judaism." In the only other passages where it occurs (Acts xxvi. 5, and James i. 26, 27), it is the rendering of the Greek θρησκεία, a word which means the outward ceremonial service of religion, the external form, as contrasted with εὐσέβεια, a word which, with one exception, is always translated *godliness* in the fifteen passages where it occurs. Θρησκεία is rendered *worshipping* in Col. ii. 18, thus plainly showing that it is outward ceremonial it implies. Its use in Acts xxvi. 5 needs no comment, but in James i. its significance is generally missed. "Pure religion," the writer declares, "is this"—and every Israelite (for to such the Epistle was specially addressed) would expect a reference to new ordinances in lieu of those of the bygone dispensation; but his thoughts turn in a wholly different direction—"to visit the fatherless and widows in their affliction, and to keep himself unspotted from the world." As Archbishop Trench remarks, the very θρησκεία of Christianity "consists in acts of mercy, of love, of holiness." The words are intended, not to indicate a parallel, but to suggest a contrast. In no more forcible and striking manner could the apostle teach that Christianity is not a θρησκεία at all.

Note 3 (page 56)

The Acts of the Apostles is divided by theologians into three main periods: The *Hebraic* (chaps.

i.–v.) ; the *Transitional* (vi.–xii.), and the *Gentile* (xiii.–xxviii.). But this classification is arbitrary. The *Hebraic* section includes at least the first nine chapters ; and if the view of the Book here advocated be correct, the rest must be regarded as *transitional.* That it is so in a real sense no student can fail to recognise ; and that this is the intention of the narrative I venture to maintain. The admission of the Gentiles, recorded in chap. x., was on strictly Jewish lines, as the apostles came to understand, and James explained at the Council of Jerusalem (xv. 13, &c.). Those that were scattered by the Stephen persecution preached " to Jews only " (xi. 19). The marginal note to ver. 20 in R.V. shows that the passage must not be strained to imply a denial of this. That Paul's ministry during the year he spent in Antioch was confined to Jews, appears from xiv. 27.[1] When from Antioch Paul and Barnabas came to Salamis " they preached in the synagogues of the Jews " (xiii. 5). When they came to Pisidian Antioch, they again repaired to the synagogue (ver. 14). And it was not till the Jews rejected the ministry that the apostles " turned to the Gentiles " (ver. 46). This passage marks one of the minor crises in the narrative. At Iconium again the apostles

[1] Because if Gentiles had been evangelised during his first visit, there would have been no need to announce on his return that God had opened the door of faith to Gentiles.

preached in the synagogue of the Jews (xiv. 1). As the "Greeks" here mentioned were attending the synagogue, they were evidently proselytes, and are not to be confounded with the "Gentiles" of verses 2 and 5. Verse 27 of the fourteenth chapter, makes it clear that Paul's ministry among the Gentiles began with his sojourn in Pisidia (chap. xiii.).

Chap. xv. claims far fuller notice than can here be given to it. Any one can see, however, that it records the session of a council of Jews to deal with new problems to which the conversion of Gentiles had given rise. Chap. xvi. 1–8 records the apostles' visits to existing Churches. The vision of ver. 9 then called them to Philippi where (as probably at Lystra) they found no synagogue. But on passing thence to Thessalonica "Paul, as his manner was," frequented the synagogue (xvii. 2). So also at Berea (ver. 10), and at Athens (ver. 17).

From Athens Paul came to Corinth where "he reasoned in the synagogue every Sabbath" (xviii. 4). So also at Ephesus (ver. 19, and xix. 8). Thence it was he turned towards Jerusalem upon that mission which is regarded by some as the fulfilment of his ministry, and by others as a turning away from the path of testimony to the Gentiles, seemingly marked out for him to follow. Be this as it may, having

been carried a prisoner to Rome, his first care
was to call together—not the Christians, much
though he longed to see them (Rom. i. 10, 11),
but—"the chief of the Jews," and to them to
give the testimony which he had brought to his
nation in every place to which his ministry had
led him. In his introductory address to them
he claimed the place of a Jew among Jews:
"I have done nothing (he declared) against the
people, or the customs of our fathers" (xxviii. 17);
but when these, the Jews of Rome, refused the
proffered mercy, his mission to his nation was at
an end; and for the first time separating himself
from them, he exclaimed, "Well spake the Holy
Ghost through Isaiah the prophet unto *your*
fathers"—and he went on to repeat the words
which our Lord Himself had used at that kindred
crisis of His ministry when the nation had openly
rejected Him (Acts xxviii. 25 R.V.; Matt. xiii. 13,
cf. xii. 14–16).

My contention is that the Acts, as a whole, is
the record of a temporary and transitional dispensation in which blessing was again offered to the
Jew and again rejected. Hence the sustained
emphasis with which the testimony to Israel is
narrated, and the incidental way in which the
testimony to Gentiles is treated. Of the thousands
baptized at Pentecost a large proportion doubtless
were of the strangers mentioned in ii. 9–11; and

these carried the testimony to the Jews in all the places there enumerated. The 5,000 men mentioned in iv. 4 were apparently resident in Jerusalem, and these, when scattered by the Stephen persecution, "went everywhere preaching the Word," "but to the Jews only" (viii. 1, 4, and xi. 19). Surely we may assume that there was not a district, not a village, inhabited by Jews, where the gospel did not come.

Some, perhaps, will appeal to passages like Acts xv. 12 to disprove my statement that miracles had special reference to the favoured nation. The careful student, however, will see that nothing in the narrative is inconsistent with what I have urged. For example, the miracle at Lystra was in response to the faith of the man who benefited by it (xiv. 9), and its effect on the heathen who witnessed it was not to lead them to Christianity, but first to make them pay Divine honour to the apostles, and then, finding they were not gods but men, to stone them. I have not said that there were no miracles wrought among the heathen, but that, when the gospel was carried to the heathen, miracles lost their prominence, and that they ceased absolutely just at the time when, if the recognised hypothesis were true, they would have been of the highest value. The great miracle of xvi. 26 was a Divine intervention on behalf of the apostle. And among the Jews of Ephesus (xix. 11) and the

Christians of Corinth (1 Cor. xii. 10) there were miracles, as doubtless elsewhere also. But there were no miracles seen by Felix or Festus or Agrippa; and, as already noticed, when Paul stood before Nero the era of miracles had closed. The miracles of Acts xxviii. 8, 9 are chronologically the last on record, and the later Epistles are wholly silent respecting them.

Note 4 (page 87)

Every one recognises that the advent of Christ marked a signal " change of dispensation," as it is termed : that is, a change in God's dealings with men. But the fact is commonly ignored that the rejection of Christ by the favoured people, and their fall in consequence from the position of privilege formerly held by them, marked another change no less definite and important (Rom. xi. 15). And yet this fact affords the solution of many difficulties and a safeguard against many errors. As indicated in these pages, it gives the clew to the right understanding of the Acts of the Apostles—a book which is primarily the record, not, as commonly supposed, of the founding of the Christian Church, but of the apostasy of the favoured nation. But it also explains much that perplexes Christians in the teaching of the Gospels.

During the last Carlist rising in Spain a wealthy

Spanish marquis was said to have mortgaged his entire estate to its utmost value, and to have thrown the proceeds into the war-chest of the insurrection. It was a reasonable act on the part of any one who believed in the Pretender's cause. To him, and to others like him, the accession of Don Carlos to the throne would bring back their own, and far more besides. So was it with the disciples in days when the kingdom was being preached to the earthly people. Certain of the Lord's precepts had reference to the special circumstances of that special dispensation. Take " the Sermon on the Mount " for example. Our Lord was there unfolding the principles of the promised kingdom, and giving precepts for the guidance of those who were awaiting its establishment. It is all for us, doubtless, but not always in the same sense that it was intended to convey to them. Christians, for instance, pray the kingdom prayer. But with us " Thy kingdom come " is a general appeal for the advancement of the Divine cause : with them it was a definite petition for the near realisation of the promised earthly reign. And what a meaning the prayer for daily bread had for those who were enjoined to carry neither purse nor scrip, but to trust their heavenly Father to feed them as He feeds the birds ; for, like the birds, they had " neither storehouse nor barn " !

Principles are unchanging, but the definite precepts recorded in such passages as Matt. v. 39–42 and vi. 25–34 were framed with reference to the circumstances of the time, and to the special testimony which the kingdom disciple was to maintain. The Christian, unlike the kingdom disciple in this respect, is entitled to defend himself against outrage, and to resist any invasion of his personal or civil rights; and he is expressly enjoined to make provision for the future. Banking, insurance, and thrift are not forbidden by Christianity. "Take nothing for your journey," the Lord directed, as He sent out the Twelve, "neither staves, nor scrip, nor bread, nor money; neither have two coats" (Luke ix. 3). And referring to this, when He was about to be taken away from them, He asked, "When I sent you without purse, and scrip, and shoes, lacked ye anything? And they said, Nothing. Then said He unto them, But now, he that hath a purse, let him take it, and likewise his scrip; and he that hath no sword, let him sell his garment and buy one" (Luke xxii. 35, 36).

What can be plainer than this? In civilised communities, of course, the State takes charge of "the sword" (Rom. xiii. 4), and the individual citizen is not left to defend himself; but the principle is the same. One who is "instructed unto the kingdom," the Lord declares, is like "a householder who brings out of his treasure things new and old" (Matt. xiii. 52). But Christians nowadays are not thus "instructed." They are rather like householders who, bringing out whatever comes first to their hand, give new milk to their guests and old wine to their babies! And as the result Holy Scripture is brought into contempt, and earnest and honest-hearted believers are stumbled or perplexed.

Another clew is needed to guide us in the right use of the teaching of the Gospels. Some of the Lord's words were addressed to the apostles *as such*, and we must remember this in applying them to ourselves.

With reference to the Sermon on the Mount it may be asked, Does any one imagine our Lord supposed that people would wish to add twenty inches to their height? Matt. vi. 27 should no doubt be read as the American Revisers render it, "Which of you by taking thought can add one cubit *to the measure of his life?*"

Note 5 (page 109)

The primary and usual meaning of μυστήριον in Biblical Greek is indicated by its use in the Septuagint. It occurs eight times in the second chapter of Daniel (verses 18, 19, 27, 28, 29, 30, 47 (twice), and again in chap. iv. 9), and in every case it is translated *secret* in our English version. The word occurs also in the Apocrypha, and always in

this same sense. This, too, is its ordinary use in the New Testament; but the word was then already acquiring the further meaning which belongs to it in the writings of the Greek Fathers, namely, a *symbol* or *secret sign*. And in this sense it appears to be used in Rev. i. 20 and xvii. 5, 7. In chap. x. 7 it occurs in its earlier meaning. So also apparently in Eph. v. 32, though the Vulgate understands it differently, using the word *sacramentum* to translate it. If it is to be read in the one way, the *secret* referred to is that believers are members of the Body of Christ: if in the other way, marriage is the *symbol* intended.

The Latin version of Eph. v. 32 is of special interest as indicating the original meaning of *sacrament*, as "a mystery; a mysterious or holy token or pledge" (Webster). Bishop Taylor thus speaks of God sending His people "the sacrament of a rainbow." And Hooker writes: "As often as we mention a *sacrament*, it is improperly under‐stood; for in the writings of the ancient fathers all articles which are peculiar to Christian faith, all duties of religion containing that which sense or natural reason cannot of itself discern, are most commonly named *sacraments*. Our restraint of the word to some few principal Divine ceremonies importeth in every such ceremony two things, the substance of the ceremony itself, which is visible; and besides that, something else more secret, in reference whereunto we conceive that ceremony to be a sacrament."

In this passage, it will be noticed, the word is used precisely in the secondary sense assigned to it in Johnson's "Dictionary," viz., "An outward and visible sign of an inward and spiritual grace." Johnson's first meaning of the word is "an oath"; and the Latin word *sacramentum* may possibly have acquired that meaning on account of some outward act or sign which accompanied the taking of an oath. According to Hooker's use of the word *sacrament*, the English practice of kissing the Testament would be so described.

Note 6 (page 118)

If the reader will take up the New Testament, and with the help of a good concordance turn to every passage where the devil is mentioned or referred to, he will be startled to find how little there is to give even a seeming support to the popular superstition upon this subject. Three passages only can I find that seem to suggest that Satan tempts to acts of immorality. Of 1 John iii. 8–10, I have already spoken. The other two are 1 Cor. vii. 5, and 1 Tim. v. 15; and with these I will deal presently.

In the temptation of our Lord there was of course no question of morality. The devil's aim was to draw Him away from the path of dependence upon

God, and specially to divert Him from the path which led to the Cross. It was this also which brought such a terrible rebuke upon Peter when the Lord addressed him as " Satan " (Matt. xvi. 23). And when Satan asked to have Peter (as he had asked to have Job) it was his *faith* he sought to destroy. " I made supplication for thee," the Lord added, " that thy *faith* fail not " (Luke xxii. 31, 32 R.V.).

And with the memory of this before him no doubt it was that the apostle wrote the words, " Your adversary the devil, as a roaring lion, walketh about, seeking whom he may devour : whom withstand stedfast in your *faith*" (1 Pet. v. 8–9). In the parable of the tares in the field, it is the devil who sows the tares (Matt. xiii. 39). And in the parable of the sower the devil's work is described as taking away the word out of the hearts of those who hear it, " lest they should *believe* and be saved." And if Elymas the sorcerer was called a " son of the devil," it was because of his " seeking to turn aside the proconsul from the faith " (Acts xiii. 8, 10).

Two passages indicate his mysterious " power of death," viz., Heb. ii. 14, and Jude 9, which tells of his claiming as of right the body of Moses. And two passages again indicate his power of inflicting disease and pain, namely, Luke xiii. 16, and Acts x. 38, but these may probably be explained by reference to the case of Job.

In Rev. xii. 9 (R.V.), he is called "the *deceiver* of the whole world" (*cf.* Rev. xx. 10) ; and in that book he is represented as the leader in the great coming struggle between faith and unfaith, between the acknowledgment of God and the denial of Him. There is no need to quote the many passages which indicate his malignant hatred of God and of His people, but if he be the obscene monster of Christian tradition, how is it that, from cover to cover, the Bible is silent on the subject? In his "devices" upon men the Satan of Scripture is the enemy, not of morals, but of *faith*.

And if in view of the mass of testimony leading to this conclusion we turn back to the two passages above cited, we shall be prepared to read them in a new light. In 1 Tim. v. we shall read verse 15 in the light of verse 12. The "turning aside after Satan" there referred to is "the setting at nought their first *faith*." And the Christian will not hesitate to follow Calvin in understanding the "faith" here intended as the faith of Christ. The word πιστὸς occurs two hundred times in the Epistles ; and in this sense only is it used, with the solitary exception of Tit. ii. 10. There is the very strongest presumption therefore against the suggestion that here it means no more than a woman's "troth" to her dead husband. Such a suggestion, moreover, makes the apostle contradict himself. It makes him say that young widows "have condemnation" because they wish to marry again; and yet he ends by expressly enjoining that they are to marry again! (ver. 14 R.V.). Verses 11–13 give his reasons for that injunction. The passage is incidentally an overwhelming condemnation of nunneries, but the usual construction put upon it is an outrage upon Holy Writ and a gross libel upon women. And I may add that if that construction were the true one the limit of age at which widows were to be provided for would certainly have been fixed much earlier than sixty.

The expressions " waxing wanton against Christ," and " turning aside after Satan," are to be explained by reference to the Scriptural standard of spiritual life and the Scriptural theology of Satanic temptations. So also of 1 Cor. vii. 5. The solemn practical lesson there to be learned is that any departure from prudence and propriety may give Satan an advantage—an occasion to undermine or corrupt the Christian's faith.

As for Ananias, his story is so misread that the lesson of it is lost to the Church. He was not a bad man, but a good man. In the enthusiasm of his zeal he sold his landed property that he might devote the proceeds to the common fund. But here the suggestion presented itself to him to put aside a portion for his own use. His wife was in the plot, and boldly lied to conceal it. But Ananias *spoke* no lie, he only acted one, as people are used to do nowadays. If he lived to-day he would be held in the highest repute. Indeed there are few to be found in these selfish days who could compare with him. The moral is not the wickedness of man but the holiness and "severity" of God, and the subtlety of Satanic temptations. Satan tempted him, not to a vicious or "immoral" act, but only to do what, as the apostle said, he had an unquestionable right to do. He did not lie to men—so the Word expressly tells us—but he lied to God, and swift judgment fell on him. If God were dealing thus with men in our day, the number of the burials would be a serious difficulty !

To the case of Judas I have not expressly referred, because it so obviously falls within the category of temptations aimed directly against Christ Himself.

Note 7 (page 123)

The exegesis here offered of John viii. 44 is not based on the grammar of the Greek article. The Revisers have adopted an unsatisfactory compromise between exposition and translation. "To speak a lie" is not English. In our language the proper expression is "to tell a lie." But no one would so render the Greek words λαλεῖν τὸ ψεῦδος ; and by inserting in the margin the old and discarded gloss, the Revisers only betray their dissatisfaction with their own reading. The words must mean either some definite lie, or else in the abstract sense the whole range of what is false. (See Psa. v. 6 LXX). In this view of the passage all speech would be regarded as divided between truth and falsehood — God-speech and devil-speech. But this is somewhat fanciful here, and, in regard to the words which follow, somewhat forced. And if, as I venture to urge, it is not the false in the abstract which is here in view, but a concrete instance of it, the question of grammar is no longer open. And, thus rendered, the connection is clear between Satan the liar and Satan the murderer. He is not the instigator to all murders, but to *the* murder there and then in question, the murder of the Christ; he is not the father of *lies*, but the father of *the* lie of which "the murder" is the natural consequence.

In Rom. i. 25, where both words ("truth" and "lie") have the article, I suppose both are used in the abstract sense. In Rev. xxi. 27 and xxii. 15 the word "lie" is anarthrous. But in 2 Thess. ii. 11 it is again *the* lie of John viii. 44. The Lawless One who is yet to be revealed, is described as he "whose coming is after the working of Satan with all power and signs and lying wonders." God does not incite men to tell lies or to believe lies. But of those who reject "*the* truth" it is written, "He shall send them strong delusion that they should believe *the* lie." Because they have rejected the Christ of God, a judicial blindness shall fall upon them that they shall accept the Christ of humanity, who will be Satan incarnate.

In these pages I have kept clear of prophecy, for they are addressed in part to those who have no belief in prophecy. But if the prophetic student will shake himself free from the Satan myth he will find the Divine forecast of the future become radiant with new light. Terrible wars are yet to convulse the nations, bringing famine in their train. But the coming Man will bring peace to the world. He will command universal homage not merely by reason of his Satanic miraculous powers, but because of his splendid human qualities. The adherents of "the truth" will, alone of all the race, have cause to mourn his sovereignty. His reign will be the era of man's "millennium," a time of order and prosperity unparalleled, when the arts of peace shall flourish, and the utopias of philosophers and socialists will be realised. And that the Satan cult which will then prevail on earth will be marked by a high morality and a specious "form of godliness," is plainly indicated by the warning that, but for Divine grace, it would "deceive the very elect." It is also, I venture to think, plainly foreshadowed by current events.

Christians are trifling with sceptical attacks upon Scripture. But the real issue involved in these attacks is the Divinity of Christ; and I venture to predict that those of us who shall live for another quarter of a century, shall yet witness a widespread abandonment of that great truth by many of the Churches. The decline of faith during the last five-and-twenty years has been appalling, and we are already within measurable distance of a more general acceptance of the Satan cult — a religion marked by a high morality and an earnest philanthropy, but wholly devoid of all that is distinctively Christian. "Free from dogma" is the favourite expression: and this "freedom" means the ignoring of the great truths of Christianity.

Note 8 (page 131)

How deep-seated and venerable is the popular belief that all misdeeds of a certain gravity are due to Satanic influence. But this belief suggests a difficulty which has perplexed and distressed many a thoughtful Christian. Multitudes innumerable thus transgress. Nor are they to be found only in the squalid dwellings of our city slums, but in the abodes of wealth and culture; not only in our great unlovely towns, but in every village and hamlet in the land. Nor are these shores in any special sense the domain of Satan On the contrary, if vice and crime are signs of his presence and power, other countries must claim more of his activity than our own. And when we turn to the darker scenes of heathenism, the appalling tale of hideous vice and cruelty gives proof that, there, the devil must be still more busy than in Christendom. But if the majority of the many thousands of millions of mankind are thus under his personal influence, he must be acquainted with the life and circumstances of each individual. Are we, then, to conclude that he is practically omnipresent and omniscient? Are we to ascribe to him these attributes of Deity?

As regards the unseen world, any belief which does not rest upon revelation is essentially superstitious : what, then, is the testimony of Scripture on this subject? The first chapter of the Epistle to the Romans treats of the condition of the heathen with a definiteness which leaves nothing to be desired. To this passage, then, let us appeal, and by it let the popular belief be tested. Here are the words :

" Knowing God, they glorified Him not as God, neither gave thanks ; but became vain in their reasonings, and their senseless heart was darkened. Professing themselves to be wise, they became fools, and changed the glory of the incorruptible God for the likeness of an image of corruptible man, and of birds, and fourfooted beasts, and creeping things. Wherefore God gave them up in the lusts of their hearts unto uncleanness, that their bodies should be dishonoured among themselves : for that they exchanged the truth of God for a lie, and worshipped and served the creature rather than the Creator, who is blessed for ever. For this cause God gave them up unto vile passions. . . . And even as they refused to have God in their knowledge, God gave them up unto a reprobate mind, to do those things which are not fitting " (Rom. i. 21–28, R.V.).[1]

If Satan were immediately responsible for the baser immoralities of men, it is inconceivable that such a passage would contain no allusion to the fact ; but allusion there is none. The words are clear and simple—" God gave them up " ; and human nature in its alienation from God accounts for their depravity. Nor will it avail to plead that it is only pagan depravity which is here in question. If no devil is needed to account for the abominations of the heathen world, why appeal to the supernatural to explain the vices and crimes of Christendom ? To do so is as unphilosophical as it is unscriptural.

And why should Satan tempt men in this way ? His doing so would be intelligible if his power over them depended on their leading vicious lives. But Scripture vetoes this suggestion. Some who own his sway are slaves of vice, but others are religious zealots of blameless character ; and our Lord ex-

[1] The whole passage from ver. 18 claims careful study. Science explains the condition of civilised man by evolution—although the only *law* it can point to is degeneracy : the rest is all mere theory— Revelation explains the state of the world generally by the fact that, having originally the knowledge of God, they wilfully lost it, and so God left them to the darkness of their own deliberate choice.

pressly declares that it is the zealots who are farthest from the kingdom.[1]

Not that immorality is any passport to heaven, any recommendation to Divine favour. On the contrary, it is a highway to " the City of Destruction " ; but it is for this very reason that it brings a man within reach of hope, for in " the City of Destruction " it is that the Saviour is seeking the lost. The devotee of blameless life, who thanks God that he is not as other men, is entirely on the devil's side ; whereas, were he tempted to open sin, he might be brought to his knees to pray that other prayer which would bring all heaven to his help.

How it would simplify matters if morality were a distinctive badge of the regenerate, and immorality characterised the rest! But vice is not the hall-mark of the devil's handiwork. " A form of godliness "[2] is one of his " devices." Among the most dangerous enemies of Christ and Christianity, are men who live pure and upright lives, and who preach righteousness. " And no marvel ; for even Satan fashioneth himself into an angel of light : it is no great thing therefore if his ministers also fashion themselves as ministers of righteousness."[3] And if " the very elect " are deceived by the fraud,

---

[1] Matt. xxi. 31.   [2] 2 Tim. iii 5.

[3] 2 Cor. xi. 14, 15 (R.V.).

it is mainly because they are blinded by this error of the Satan myth.

It is not, I again repeat, in the domain of morals that the devil's influence is distinctively declared, but in the spiritual sphere. Our race has not sprung from Adam in Eden innocence, but from Adam the fallen and sinful outcast. Human nature is thus poisoned at its very source by ignorance and distrust of God. It is a *fallen* nature. And Satan it was who thus debased it. What wonder, then, that he is able to influence the main currents of human thought and action in regard to things Divine! What wonder that he can control the religion of the race!

All this may excite the contempt of the agnostic, but we challenge him to offer some other explanation of the well-ascertained facts. The evolutionist pretends to account for the condition of the lower strata of humanity ; but how can he explain the phenomena of the religion of Christendom ? In spite of all the advantages which civilisation affords, men have bartered the sublime truths of Christianity for the superstitions of old-world paganism. Such figments as baptismal regeneration and the possession of mystic powers by a priestly caste are wholly repugnant to Christianity, and Judaism, even in its apostasy, was free from them ; and yet they have been adopted as an integral part of the Christian religion. This one fact is proof that, so far at least as the origin of man is concerned, evolution is false and the story of the Eden fall is true.

But this kind of Satanic influence involves no knowledge of the inner experience of each life, no possession of Divine attributes. It implies no special action directed simultaneously against millions of individuals scattered over all the globe. That the devil does deal with individuals we know; but Scripture indicates that such cases are exceptional. The warning to the Twelve, that Satan desired to have them, though intended for all, was specially for Peter. It is but natural that he should seek to drag down those who stand out as champions of the truth. Nor can even the lowliest disciple be sure of immunity from his attacks. He "walketh about," we read, "as a roaring lion, seeking whom he may devour." [1] And a prowling lion may seize even the very weakest for his prey. This may explain conflicts which sometimes try the faith even of the humblest Christian.

The old classification of "the world, the flesh, *and* the devil" is a right one. And "our *wrestling* is not against flesh and blood." [2] In the "flesh" sphere our safety is in flight. But flight from Satan is impossible. "Flee youthful lusts;" [3] but "Resist the devil, and he will flee from you." [4] Such is the

[1] 1 Pet. v. 8.
[2] Eph. vi. 12 (R.V.).
[3] 2 Tim. ii. 22.
[4] James iv. 7.

distinction clearly marked in Scripture. The baser "lusts of the flesh" are entirely under a man's control, unless indeed he is enervated by vicious indulgence ; but with the strongest and holiest of men "the whole armour of God" is the only sure defence against the attacks of Satan.[1]

Of the devil's aim and methods I have already spoken. No one, I repeat, may assert that he might not use the basest means to ensnare a minister of Christ, and thus mar his testimony and destroy his usefulness. But it cannot be asserted too often or too plainly that his normal effort is not to tempt to the commission of sins such as lead to contrition, and teach us how weak we are ; but, by drawing us away to mere human morality, or religion, or philosophy, to deaden or destroy our sense of dependence upon God. For sin may humble a Christian ; but human philosophy and religion can only foster his self-esteem. And pride is "the snare of the devil" ;[2] not humility.

That there are "unclean spirits" we know. And certain abnormal phases of depravity may be due possibly, even in our own day, to demoniacal possession ; but this is wholly distinct from Satanic temptations. And demons even are not all "unclean." The warned-against "teachings of demons" in "later times" are not incitements to vice, but to a more exacting morality

---

[1] Eph. vi. 11.   [2] 1 Tim. iii. 6, 7.

and a spirituality more transcendental than even Christianity enjoins. Marriage itself is repulsive to this fastidious cult, and certain kinds of food, "which God created to be received with thanksgiving," it absolutely rejects.[1]

The flagrant immoralities of some of the Corinthian converts drew from the apostle no suggestion of Satanic agency, save indeed as a possible means towards the restoration of those who had sinned.[2] The warning, "Lest Satan should get an advantage of us," was given when their zeal to clear themselves betrayed them into resentment against the offenders.[3] And it was the advent of false teachers "preaching another Jesus" which evoked the further warning against the Serpent's "subtilty," lest their minds should be "corrupted from the simplicity that is in Christ."[4] So again, when persecution prevailed in the Thessalonian church, he was solicitous "to know their faith," fearing "lest the Tempter should tempt them," and their confidence in God should fail.

There is one passage of Scripture which some seem to think refutes what has been here maintained. As a matter of fact it may be appealed to

---

[1] See 1 Tim. iv. 1–4. It may be noticed here in passing that during recent years, both in Europe and America, these doctrines have been insidiously taught by certain spiritualists, who commend their teaching by seemingly pure and blameless lives.

[2] 1 Cor. v. 1–5.   [3] 2 Cor. ii. 11.

[4] 2 Cor. xi. 3, 4.

in support of it. The following are the opening words of the second chapter of Ephesians :

> "And you did He quicken, when ye were dead through your trespasses and sins, wherein aforetime ye walked according to the course of this world, according to the prince of the power of the air, of the spirit that now worketh in the sons of disobedience ; among whom we also all once lived in the lusts of our flesh, doing the desires of the flesh and of the mind, and were by nature children of wrath, even as the rest " (Eph. ii. 1–3, R.V.).

Those who read this passage in the light of the Satan myth entirely lose its special teaching. The life of every unregenerate man, whether marked by the grossest vice or by high morality, by utter atheism or by intense religious zeal, is " according to the spirit that worketh in the sons of disobedience." The life of Saul the persecutor had been as pure and blameless as was the life of Paul the apostle of the Lord. And yet he here brackets himself with the Ephesian converts. Hence the emphatic " *all* " of the third verse. All alike had walked " according to the prince of the power of the air," and therefore " according to the course of this world," for Satan is this world's prince and god.[1] So far from implying that their " trespasses and sins " had been due to supernatural incitement, the apostle expressly declares they had been altogether natural and human. The Gentile sensualists were but " doing the desires of

[1] John xiv. 30, xvi. 11 ; 2 Cor. iv. 4.

the flesh"; the Jewish zealot "the desires of the mind."[1]

For the terms immorality and sin are not convertible. The one refers to an arbitrary human standard of right; the other to a standard altogether Divine. As already indicated,[2] the essence of sin is *lawlessness*. Man was endowed by his Creator with a will absolutely free. But, though all blessing depended on his keeping it in subjection, he asserted it in opposition to the Divine will. And as the result "the carnal (or natural) mind is enmity against God; for (as the apostle adds) it is not subject to the law of God, neither indeed can be."[3] Our fallen nature has thus become subject to its own law of gravitation; and it would be as unreasonable to expect a man to achieve the physical feat of mounting upward towards the sky, as to suppose that, apart from Divine grace, the life of an unregenerate sinner could turn Godward. In the one case as in the other, a miracle alone could account for the phenomenon. And such a miracle both

---

[1] In the N.T. "the flesh" means usually either the body, or bodily nature, of man, or else human nature as a whole in its fallen and corrupt condition. But in Eph. ii. 3 it is contrasted with "the mind," and therefore it appears to mean man's corrupt *bodily* nature. In Eph. i. 18 and iv. 18 (as also in I John v. 20), διάνοια is translated "understanding." (In i. 18 the R.V. reads καρδία.) St. Paul uses the word *flesh* in different senses even in the same passage; see Eph. ii. 3, 11, 15, *ex. gr.*

[2] Pp. 120–121 *ante.*   [3] Rom. viii. 7.

the apostle himself and the Ephesian converts had experienced. Hence the added words :— "But God, being rich in mercy, for His great love wherewith He loved us, even when we were dead through our trespasses, quickened us together with Christ." [1] No miracle, indeed, is needed to enable men to lead moral and religious lives. Here the words of Enid's song are true :—

"For man is man, and master of his fate." [2]

It is in the *spiritual* sphere that, by the law of his nature, he ever gravitates downward, and falls away from God.

Finally, I would again remark that the Christian who turns to prophecy with a mind unbiased by traditional views about Satan will find new meaning in the predictions relating to the "latter days." Delegated authority was all the devil claimed in the Temptation, as appears from the very words he used. To him, he declared, had been "delivered" the kingdoms of the world, with all the power and the glory of them.[3] But the power and the glory the Christian has been taught to ascribe to God alone. In his last great effort, therefore, Satan incarnate will claim to be Divine.[4] And the lie, we are told, will be accredited by " all power and signs and lying wonders." [5] God's " millen-

[1] Eph. ii. 4, 5 (R.V.).   [2] " Idylls of the King."   [3] Luke iv. 6.
[4] 2 Thess. ii. 4.   [5] 2 Thess. ii. 9.

nium " will be anticipated and travestied by the reign of the Man of Sin. And the fact that the devil will yield to him " his throne and great authority " [1] has led to the assumption that his rule will be marked by Saturnalian orgies of violence and lust. But how, then, can we explain the words of Christ, that the world will hail him as the true Messiah, and that, if such a thing were possible, the very elect would be deceived by the imposture ? [2] If read with a right appreciation of the Satan of Scripture, these words of our Divine Lord are a most solemn warning to the believer, even for the days we live in ; but read in the false light of the Satan myth, they remain an insoluble enigma.

Note 9 (page 144)

According to English law " the Lord's day "— as Sunday is designated in the old statutes— is a day on which no judge or magistrate may sit, and no jury may be empanelled. The criminal may be taken red-handed, but all that the law can do is to hold him in ward until the day of grace has run its course, and a competent tribunal may adjudicate upon his crime. If our law went further in the same direction, and the functions of the constable also were suspended, it would

[1] Rev. xiii. 2 (R.V.).
[2] Matt. xxiv. 24. See pp. 188–189 *ante.*

afford an apter illustration of the great truth that is here in question. But to make the parable complete, we must go even further still, and suppose not only that the criminal enjoys for the moment freedom even from arrest, but that there is an amnesty in force by which he may secure absolute immunity from all the consequences of his crime.

But to hold such language is to speak in an unknown tongue ; and to turn to the words of Scripture in support of it is to risk losing men's attention altogether. The mystery of the gospel is that God can *justify* a sinner, and yet be just. He justifies the *ungodly*. "To him that worketh not, but believeth in Him that justifieth the ungodly, his faith is counted for righteousness" (Rom. iv. 5). Here is another kindred statement : "The grace of God hath appeared salvation-bringing to all men." And the passage proceeds : "For we also were aforetime foolish, disobedient, deceived, serving divers lusts and pleasures, living in malice and envy, hateful, hating one another. But when the kindness of God our Saviour, and His love-toward-man, appeared, not by works done in righteousness, which we did ourselves, but according to His mercy He saved us" (Tit. ii. 11–14, and iii. 3–5). Or if any would wish to have words spoken by the lips of our blessed Lord Himself, they will be found in many a passage of the Gospels. Here, for example, is His testimony to Nicodemus : " For God so loved the world, that He gave His only begotten Son, that whosoever believeth in Him should not perish, but have everlasting life."

Are we not justified, then, in saying that forgiveness and eternal life are brought within reach of all ; that heaven is made as free to sinful men as infinite love and grace can make it ? If words have any meaning, this, and nothing less than this, is the truth. But how is this gospel treated? In the minds of the religious it excites the utmost indignation. They no longer burn men at the stake for proclaiming it, as in darker days they used to do, but though their anger shows itself in gentler ways it is just as real. And upon common men it makes no impression whatever. A man once stood on London Bridge, for a wager, offering real sovereigns for a shilling each. The notice he displayed was plainly worded, and it was read by hundreds of the passers-by. But by all it was read incredulously, and therefore with indifference. He won his wager : not a single coin was taken from him ! And for the same reason " the gospel of the grace of God " is ignored. It will be thus ignored by hundreds who will read these pages. Men are possessed by the belief that eternal life can be attained only upon impracticable conditions, and so their attitude towards the whole matter is one of apathy. But apathy gives place to anger if any one dares to speak of eternal judgment and a hell for the impenitent. No blasphemy can be too daring to hurl at a God who would not bring a sinner to heaven in the way that a constable brings a drunken prisoner to the lock-up—without his will, or, if needs be, *against* his will!

But man, made in the image of God, is endowed with a will, and to that will the Divine appeal is addressed. "Ye *will not* come to Me that ye might have life" was the Lord's yearning intreaty to those who listened to His words, but refused to give heed to them. "Whosoever *will*, let him take the water of life freely." God's own heaven is the home to which He is calling sinful men. Hell has been prepared, not for such, but for the devil and his angels. But if men refuse Christ and take sides with Satan, they must reap what they sow.

Note 10 (page 153)

"Of what value, then, is prayer?" some one will ask, and "What place is there for it?" It is with extreme diffidence that I venture to give expression to thoughts on this subject which have long taken possession of my own mind. And I do so only because it may possibly bring relief to many who are sorely distressed at the seeming failure of the prayer-promises of the Gospels. Words could not be plainer than those in which our Lord impressed on His disciples that Almighty power was absolutely at their disposal, if only they had faith. When they wondered that the fig-tree withered at His word, He told them that they too could command this, or even the moving of a mountain. And He added, " And all things whatsoever ye shall ask in prayer, believing, ye shall receive " (Matt. xxi. 20–22). How many there are who in intensest earnestness have claimed such promises, and have reaped bitter disappointment which has staggered their faith! It is easy of course to explain the failure by reading into the promise conditions of one kind or another, though the Lord Himself made no conditions whatever. But instead of tampering thus with His words, let us consider whether the true solution of the difficulty may not be found in the truth which these pages have endeavoured to unfold.

And here the striking fact claims attention that while the record of the Pentecostal dispensation presents us with the practical counterpart of all such promises, the Epistles, which unfold the doctrine of the present dispensation, and describe the life which befits that doctrine—the life of faith — inculcate thoughts about prayer which are essentially different, and which are entirely in accord with the actual experience of spiritual Christians.[1]

Some perhaps may urge that while the earlier Gospels may thus be explained, *St. John* cannot be treated in this way. I can in reply but plead with the thoughtful reader to consider whether every word addressed to the apostles is intended to apply to all believers at all times. Take John xiv. 12 as a test of this. Is every believer to be endowed with miraculous powers equal to or greater than those exercised by the Lord Himself? We are prepared at once to limit the scope of such words : is it so clear, then, that the words which immediately follow are of universal application? We have the fact, I repeat, that both these promises were proved to be true in the Pentecostal dispensation, and that neither has been proved to be true in the Christian Church.[2] So also of chap. xv. 16, and of xvi. 23, &c.

But, it will be asked, Is not the promise explicitly repeated in St. John's First Epistle (1 John iii. 22 and v. 14, 15)? I think not. It seems to me that the apostles were *in a special sense* empowered both

[1] James v. 13 may seem to be an exception. But without raising the question where " the Elders of the Church " are to be found in our day, it may suffice to notice that this Epistle, being expressly addressed to *Israel* (chap. i. 1), belongs dispensationally to the Pentecostal era, which will be renewed when Israel is restored.

[2] See Chap. V. *ante.* I am convinced that they will be equally true in a dispensation which is still future ; but I do not enter on such topics here.

to act and to pray in the name of the Lord Jesus, whereas the Christian should bow in presence of the words, "according to His will." As Dean Alford here remarks, "If we knew His will thoroughly, and submitted to it heartily, it would be impossible for us to ask anything, for the spirit or for the body, which He should not hear and perform. And it is this ideal state, as always, which the apostle has in view." But the Christian too commonly makes his own longings, or his supposed interests, and not the Divine will, the basis of his prayer; he goes on to persuade himself that his request will be granted; he then regards this "faith" as a pledge that he has been heard; and finally, when the issue belies his confident hopes, he gives way to bitterness and unbelief. True faith is always prepared for a refusal. Some, we read, "through faith," "obtained promises"; but, no less "through faith," "others were tortured, not accepting deliverance."

Some, perhaps, may think it a sufficient refutation of all this to appeal to what are called "striking answers to prayer," such as certain Christians have experienced in every age. But the appeal refutes itself. They are justly regarded as "*striking* answers" precisely because they are exceptional. No one may dare to limit what God will do for the believer. But to make the experience of some the standard of faith for all is one of the greatest errors and snares of Christian life. If these promises are of universal application, the fact that any answer to prayer should be considered striking in any sense is proof of general apostasy.

A detailed examination of the passages in the Epistles which refer to this subject would far exceed the limits of a note. One more may suffice. I allude to the familiar words of Phil. iv. 6, 7 : " In nothing be anxious ; but in everything by prayer and supplication with thanksgiving let your requests be made known unto God. And the peace of God, which passeth all understanding, shall guard your hearts and your thoughts in Christ Jesus" (R.V.). It is a solemn thing to make unconditioned demands upon God. To the record of such prayers may often be added the solemn words : " He gave them their request, but sent leanness into their soul." Hezekiah prayed in this way. He claimed a prolongation of his life, and God granted his petition; and the added years gave him his son Manasseh, and the consequences of Manasseh's sin (that God " would not pardon ") still rest as a blight and a curse upon that nation ! Such a prayer, I make bold to say, is unfitting to the Christian. How different the teaching of the Divine Spirit ! It may be the life of husband or wife, of parent or child, that is in the balance : what then shall be the believer's attitude ? To claim it, as Hezekiah did, and chance

the awful risks which the answer may entail? Or
"by prayer and supplication with thanksgiving,"
to leave the request with God ; and having thus left
it all with Him, to trust His love and wisdom with
the issue? It was thus the apostle prayed, when
he sought relief from that mysterious hindrance to
his ministry ; and the denial of his request, instead
of bringing bitterness of soul, only served to teach
him more of "the power of Christ" (2 Cor. xii.
8, 9). Above all it was thus the Master prayed in
the garden of Gethsemane (Matt. xxvi. 39, 42).

The prayer of the Pentecostal age was like
drawing cheques to be paid in coin over the
counter. The prayer of the Christian dispensation—that is, of the life of faith—is to make known
our requests to God, and to be at peace. If the
matter were one within the power of a friend
to deal with—a friend whose wisdom we could
trust and of whose love we were assured—should
we not be content to say, after telling him all,
"Now you know my feelings and my wishes, and
I leave the case entirely in your hands." And this
is just what God invites.

Note 11 (page 160)

The sceptic seldom admits that any position
once held by him is untenable, and a signal exception to this is deserving of special notice. Not

content with making havoc of the Old Testament, criticism has long been " running amuck " through the New Testament also. " It has been demonstrated " (says a recent writer) " that the selection of the books composing it and their separation from the vast mass of spurious gospels, epistles, and apocalyptic literature was a gradual process, and, indeed, that the rejection of some books and the acceptance of others was accidental." [1] But all this is now exploded by the greatest living authority upon the subject, Professor Harnack of Berlin. And his testimony is all the more telling because he gives no sign of repentance as regards his utter rejection of Christianity. Himself the foremost champion of unorthodoxy, he freely owns that in this matter the critics are wrong and the orthodox are right. Here is an extract from the preface to his recent work on " The Chronology of the oldest Christian Literature " :

[1] Mr. Andrew D. White's " Warfare of Science with Theology," vol. ii. p. 388. This writer's appointment to the American Embassy at Berlin will no doubt call increased attention to his book. Real forensic skill is apparent in the use he makes of his great erudition ; for, allowing for one important omission, his work is quite encyclopedic. His indictment of "theology" is overwhelming, and with much of it I am of course in thorough sympathy. But of *Christianity*, so far as appears from his treatise, he knows absolutely nothing. To him our Divine Lord is merely " the Blessed Founder " of the Christian religion—the Buddha of Christendom. Indeed he belongs to that large class of persons who, without offence, may be aptly described as Christianised Buddhists.

" There was a time—the general public indeed has not got beyond it—in which the oldest Christian literature, including the New Testament, was looked upon as a tissue of deceptions and forgeries. That time is passed. For science it was an episode in which it learned much, and after which it has much to forget. The results, however, of the following investigations go in a 'reactionary' direction, beyond what can be described as the middle position of present-day criticism. The oldest Literature of the Church in all main points and in most details, from the point of view of literary criticism, is genuine and trustworthy. In the whole New Testament there is in all probability only a single writing which can be looked upon as pseudonymous in the strictest sense of the word—*i.e.*, the Second Epistle of Peter."

This is but one of many proofs that the tide has turned which in recent years has threatened to undermine the Christian faith. In the scepticism of the day there is nothing distinctive save that so many of its champions are men who are publicly pledged and subsidised to teach what they deny. It is only the unstable and the ignorant who are overwhelmed by a book like that above cited.[1] Neither the well-instructed nor the spiritual can be thus led to reject the Bible as a fraud and

[1] " Warfare of Science with Theology."

Christianity as a superstition. They can understand the difference between a Divine revelation
and human comments and commentaries. To
take a single example—they do not regard the
Ussher-Lloyd Chronology in the margin of our
English Bible as " equally inspired with the sacred
text itself." [1] And while refusing to accept open-
mouthed the wild conjectures of certain Egypto-
logists as to the antiquity of ancient dynasties, they
recognise that the " conjectural periods " between
the Deluge and the Kingdom must be largely
extended.

If we eliminate the blunders of theologians and
" reconcilers " on the one hand and the *theories*
(as distinguished from the facts) of science on the
other, a ponderous treatise like Mr. A. D. White's
would be reduced to very small proportions. The
whole " Mosaic Cosmogony " controversy is ruled
out at once, and many questions which seem of
serious moment shrink into the background or
entirely disappear. Moreover, there is in Holy
Scripture a " hidden harmony " unknown to those
who ignore the scheme of type and prophecy
which permeates the whole. This study is a sure
antidote to scepticism. No student of prophecy
is a sceptic. And as regards the typology of
Scripture, which is the alphabet of the language

[1] " Warfare of Science with Theology," vol. i. p. 253.

in which the New Testament is written, there is not one of the rationalists who has given proof of possessing any knowledge whatever. Ignorance of the alphabet is a fatal defect in those who claim to expound the text; and this ignorance, which Hengstenberg deplored in his day, is still absolute in the case of all without exception who are seeking to prove that the Bible is but a human book. "Truth brings out the hidden harmony, when unbelief can only, with a dull dogmatism, deny."

INDEX